Paul Hanford is a writer, podcast[...] was born in Dorset, England in [...] was part of Brothers In Sound, w[...] released three EPs and an LP, *Family Is For Sharing*, on Parlophone/Regal between 1998–2001. He released several records as Sancho before studying Music Culture Theory at UEL. Moving to London, he spent ten years working as a music consultant, being a full-time DJ in bars and events across London, as well as presenting radio and TV on Hoxton Radio and London Live.

He moved to Berlin in 2018 with an award from the Arts Council of England and set up the Lost and Sound podcast. Publications he's written for include *Wired*, *Huck*, *DJMag*, *Mixmag*, *Borshch*, Beatportal, Boiler Room and Somesuch Stories.

COMING
TO
BERLIN

Global journeys into an
electronic music and club
culture capital

PAUL HANFORD

First published by Velocity Press 2022

velocitypress.uk

Printed and bound in Great Britain by Clays Ltd, Elcograf S.p.A.

Cover design
Hayden Russell

Cover image
Nina Richards

Typesetting
Paul Baillie-Lane
pblpublishing.co.uk

ISBN: 9781913231156

CONTENTS

ACKNOWLEDGEMENTS

My biggest thanks and love to my parents. An equally huge appreciation to everyone who trusted me to share parts of their life here: Mark Reeder, Danielle DePicciotto, Farhad, Alan Oldham, Gerald Simpson, Zoe Angelina, Joseph Kamaru, Thomas Tichai, Alexandre Decoupigny, Ziúr, Robert Bennett, Julia Küchler, Sonia Fernández Pan, Paul Hockenos, David Jazay, Alexander Hacke.

Thank you deeply to Colin Steven at Velocity Press for stepping up and being solid. And to friends and colleagues, some helping directly, some who may not even be aware they helped me. In no particular order: Gaby D'Annunzio, Laura Jean Marsh, Tena Strok, Ben Osborn, Tom Giddins, Kathleen and Sly, Adam and Vanessa, Markus Nikolaus, Tim Lawrence and Helen Reddington, Kianí Del Valle, Ed Dowie, Emma T, Tom Haines, Dora Pan, Laura Jefcoate, Agata Smith, Emma Robertson, Fabien Riggall, Gerd Grauer, Estela Oliva, Tom Haines, Antonio Cárdenas, Robert Henke, Obar Ejimiwe, Portrait XO, Dirk Molt, Russ Kemp, Tom Greatorex, Laura Little, Dream Baby Dream, No Shade, Igor Condric, Juta, Johana, the people who work at and run Tischendorf, Sankt Oberholtz, Chapter One, Cafe Mu, Leutchstoff, Laidak, The Visit, Jorgan Borg, Kerrie Robinson, Valdone Porcheddu, Marge Goymer.

If I've forgotten you, my apologies – I'll buy you a jar of pickled onions or something.

PREFACE

Coming To Berlin was written between August 2021 and February 2022. It was begun in a Neukölln *Altbau*, and then the majority was written in winter in Friedrichshain and in cafes across the city. But the first seeds came earlier when I finally moved to Berlin in 2018.

Prior, after each stay, I'd return back to London with a reignited passion for electronic music and a deep sense that there is still a place in the world where outsiders are not only accepted but help define, as well as run the electricity, on a city's cultural power. Over the following few years, every time I'd visit, whether I danced or not, I bathed in that feeling of acceptance, of myself and of others, and of feeling comfortable in my own skin. A sense of freedom, as punk as it is techno, as anarchic as it is ambient, kept manifesting in daily interactions, in graffiti, in places I'd go, cafes, lakes, the U-Bahn, wherever.

In March 2018, grappling with my own Britishness during a time of Brexit that left me feeling alienated from a society that could decide to leave Europe, I felt it was now or never. I applied for an Arts Council grant, which to my surprise, I got. The brief? Research Berlin's music culture. I moved into a WG in Friedrichshain, the first of fourteen places I've lived in the city so far. I interviewed DJs and producers, musicians, historians, promoters and activists. The idea was that this could form a book, but instead, it became the beginning of the ongoing podcast, Lost and Sound.

For several years, the idea of writing a book about Berlin's music culture stuck with me, but I was held back by imposter syndrome. Why the fuck should I, a newcomer, an *Ausländer*, get to write about someone else's culture? Shouldn't it be written by somebody who has been in the scene since before the Wall fell, at the very least? But then it hit me: so many creative people in Berlin are the same as me. They were, at one point, newcomers too. And this is exactly what Berlin represents to so many that have come here from all across the world: a place where we hope to express our identities. It's an island of individuality in a sea of commercialisation. The driving force behind this is way deeper than electronic music and the dancefloor, but for so many of us who were at one point new here, this is our starting point.

Coming To Berlin isn't a straightforward book about electronic music and club culture. Many of the city's big names appear only as references, cameos in the lives of the people I met. Instead, I've written a book where music is a soundtrack to how a city can provide, or even not provide, a cultural home for artists and outsiders. Each chapter is an encounter, and it's as much about the city itself as it is the amazing people I met.

This book is, in part, a plea to treat the city with respect. A lot is at stake right now; the tide of gentrification is creeping in. Rents have risen over 70% in the last decade; communities are being displaced. Plus, on the day I write this, 14 February 2022 (eerily enough, ten years to the day since I first set my foot down off that Easyjet into Flughafen Schönefeld), clubs, the city's long-running heartbeat, are only just gearing up to reopen. The absence has been felt significantly, businesses have closed, everything has been affected, and this brings me to one more thing: I decided not to hide the pandemic from the narratives.

I've written this equally for people anywhere fascinated to learn more about electronic music culture and the dance-floor as I have for those, like myself, who live here. The book is deeply personal; to some, this book may not even seem to be about clubbing at all. This is a book about Berlin, or rather, this is a book about my version of Berlin, experienced through moments I've shared with people you'll meet over the following pages.

Paul Hanford
Berlin, 14 February 2022

1.

FRESH SNOW ON RIGAER STRASSE
INTRODUCTION. ARRIVALS.

The first time I danced in Berlin was in a place I never knew the name of, and in the years since, I have never found where it was.

I remember conversations; I remember the lights, the frequencies, movement. I even remember the hair and voices of the people I crammed into a taxi with on the way there and the position of the warped Formica tables stacked with coats and bags that had been shoved around the side of the dancefloor. Most significantly, I remember dancing and the feeling emitting out between everyone, and that it wasn't just one thing. Maybe I'd glimmered this feeling sporadically before, a moment at a festival perhaps, forgotten moments in fields rekindled unexpectedly. Over the following month, that feeling extended outwards into my experiences of being in the city, a few more times as I danced but more than that. In cafes, in bars, in the tempo of conversations, with the way strangers would look at each other. Sometimes gruff. Sometimes flirtatious. Rude or sexy. Warm or cold. It was an energy I couldn't and didn't want to define. I just wanted to be in it. What I don't

1

remember, because maybe I never knew to begin with, is the club's name.

I remember the beginning of the night. Twisted half out of the window ledge, the snow falling across the tenement courtyard. I checked the list of places Maya recommended. Bars mostly, nothing too hectic; I was exhausted and wanted to ease my way in. That afternoon we'd eaten bagels and stove coffee standing up by the fridge as we both drew up comparative lists. Not long after, wiping crumbs from her lips, she wrapped into a thick black scarf until her neck disappeared, lifting a travel bag over her shoulder. I opened the front door, and with a draft of cold air, she said what I'd later realise was not cheers but *tschuss*. Bye.

This was my first night alone in Berlin. I'd arrived earlier in the week, 14 February 2012. Maya was a friend of a friend and we'd arranged a room swap. She was studying and wanted to write her thesis and cycle around Hackney. I didn't know what a Berghain was, or a Tresor, and the only Sisyphos I knew was a myth. Still, the prospect of spending a winter month living in her Friedrichshain *Altbau* played into this romantic notion I'd built up from years of listening to *Low*, *Heroes* and *Lodger*, those three albums Bowie made in the two years he lived across town in Schöneberg. To me, that meant a sort of desolate isolation and creative rebirth. Historically neglectful perhaps, but something I'd come to learn I was very far from unique in feeling.

In London, I had once been an electronic music producer. I worked in events and then, through this, I'd become a DJ, but not a DJ in the sense of what I'd reconnect with over that night and in the months and years following. I was a DJ in the sense that I'd figure out what to play to different clients. And then I'd play it in an order I'd figure most effective, and this would get me bookings. I played film wrap parties and weddings, bars, openings and hotels. I played requests. Sometimes I'd finish one set, Pret sandwich in one hand, headphones dangling, straight onto the tube to the next. Fun. Formula but fun. Rent paid. But hang on a minute – really, I just like to make things. I like to make connections, and I'd forgotten this somewhere along the way. Maya and I started talking through Messenger about her little one-room apartment, and that in February, Berlin would be really cold – like, really cold. I could spend time in a city where I didn't know anyone and didn't speak the language. I thought of 'A New Career In A New Town' off Bowie's *Low*. I played the track on repeat, those wintry synths, the distant harmonica that sounds like a drunk making their way home along a brutalist alleyway. Maya had some fantasies about London too. Over a month of Facebook conversations, it felt a trust had been built. We arranged the room swap.

The first several days, I trudged in the snow along Simon-Dach-Straße. I found a thrift store; my London shoes had holes and my socks turned into a soggy mess. I bought some trainers for ten euros and ate lunch in the first place I saw. I ordered something off a menu I didn't understand and went to Mitte, spending an afternoon reading a book in Café Cinema on Hackescher Markt. And I slept. I slept a lot. I had absolutely no desire to do anything other than just slow down. In the evenings, Maya would get back from her student job. One night we went to what I'd come to know as Kotti, where Maya introduced the concept of Club-Mate in the smoky backroom of Cafe Luzia.

It tasted like herbal Irn-Bru, and at the bar, they topped up our litre bottles with vodka. We went up a graffiti-covered stairwell and listened to a DJ playing New Order in Paloma Bar. Maya taught me some very rudimentary Deutsch, and that one of the first words *Ausländers* like myself start using is *genau*, which sort of means 'I agree.' She joked that *Ausländers* will often, if they don't understand what a German has just said, reply with a simple *genau*. Another: *Kann ich bitte einen Wodka haben*? And then I'd go and try saying this at the bar.

On the Saturday after Maya left, I showered and went for a walk around the neighbourhood. The snow along Rigaer Straße fell so consistently that in those first few days I never noticed the cobbled paving. I stopped off at Lidl; it was Saturday evening, and she'd warned me that supermarkets shut on Sunday. 'So unless you want to live off Haribo from the *Späti*,' she'd said, 'go before you go out.' I asked her what a *Späti* was and she described to me the little Turkish-ran late shops where you can buy alcohol, tobacco, snacks and maybe toilet roll. There I was, learning the rudimentary *Ausländer* terms. *Späti*. Kotti. *Genau*.

On the way, along Rigaer Straße, I saw protest banners hanging from balconies. Years later, I'd get told these were once unoccupied buildings. During a period after the Wall fell, in what the publisher Christoph Links called 'The Wonderful Year of Anarchy', these buildings became the squatted housing of young East Berliners and their wealthier West German cousins. There were battles between occupants and the police. 'The Battle of Mainzer Straße'. I'd also learned that a decade before the battles, inside a church I'd pass on my way back from Lidl, in the tall and Gothic Samariterkirche, a union formed between young East German punks and the Catholic church, right under the radar of the Stasi.

I got back, ate and opened the kitchen window, looking at the list of bars and clubs in the area Maya had recommended. At the top: Berghain. This word came up in conversation more and more. 'You can even walk to it from here,' she suggested. I gulped. In my years out of sync with underground dance culture, there was a lot to catch up on, and so what if people were saying that this big old former factory was the best club in the world? An opinion was setting in my tired mind: stringent door policy and strict minimalism. Fucking on the dancefloor and The Piss Man in the urinals. You've got to wear black. Yada yada. Even now, even amongst Berliners, Berghain gets mentioned so often in the hyperbolic, an invitation to recount wild experiences. And at that moment, smoking out of the window, tired, and as I practised saying *Kann ich bitte einen Wodka haben?* and *genau* into the night air, it just sounded too much. An hour later, I was in Süss War Gestern.

On the way, snow was a blizzard, Simon-Dach-Straße eerily quiet. In the decade following, I would only again feel this overwhelming quietness during lockdown. I passed Astro bar, the long-gone KPTN, the Intimes Cinema. Left along Wühlischstraße. Maya had described Süss War Gestern as a bar but with a club atmosphere. So I think, hey, I can listen to DJs, maybe even dance, but then leave at a reasonable hour and be in bed early. *Genau*. I found a seat near the DJ booth, cigarette smoke ascending into swirly grey constellations around dozens of miniature disco balls, and I asked someone what the bar's name was in English: Sweet Was Yesterday. Inside the

DJ booth, a woman with blonde frizzy hair was taking over from a guy in a beanie hat. She had her headphones hanging below her chin and used fingers delicately to cue in a record. Backwards a little. Pause. A little forward.

'Hey, what do you think?' says a voice, leaning over from a group of five or six next to me. 'We're debating if midnight is too early to go to Berghain.' They've all driven down from Oslo, crossing the Baltic Sea via the ferry; we chinked glasses. I tell them I'm new in town too, but that I'd heard locals go on Sunday morning. Maybe eleven. 'Eleven in the morning?' said one, with an air of exasperation. It's funny how I remember her peeling the label on a bottle of beer, saying how she didn't think she could stay awake so long, their warmth as they invited me into their circle and that Nordic ability to naturally switch on English mannerisms. I remember all this, but what I don't remember are their names. Or even particularly what they looked like. We drink, and every now and again debate whether to go or not. We jump into a taxi.

The taxi pulls up and I see it for the first time, like a giant radiator standing in the middle of industrial scrubland. An austere workhouse in DDR cream with a long line of people reaching outwards in black, beyond where a man is stood by a fridge on wheels, selling bottles of beer. As the years pass, I will meet people for whom being inside this factory at the weekends is a way of life. People who adjust their diet so that they can have both adequate stamina and recovery. I will know people who live deliberately within walking distance. I will have a friend who, after one night inside, moved here from Melbourne. When federal policy towards the pandemic altered in the autumn of 2021 and the club reopened for several months, it was not uncommon to stand in this line for seven hours. And what's more, some people will tell me that the queueing is not only worth it but forms part of the process of leaving behind the world you've spent the rest of the week in. After maybe an hour, we had reached an inner courtyard, off the industrial estate, where a cattle grid folds inwards towards the rattling bass of a kick drum. We huddle together, drunk and talking loudly, edging nearer the entrance.

It's then that I saw groups walking away from the door, back past the cattle grid and out towards the darkness of Friedrichshain. 'They didn't get in,' one of my new friends said. How strange, these people looked clean, presentable. They looked exactly how you'd look to get into clubs, I thought. Then, we're at the front. A tall, grey-bearded figure with a tattoo on the side of his face looked at me calmly, his eyes directing me across the other side of the line. For a second, as I walked with my new friends into a shadowy corner, I thought that maybe there were two entrances. But then I realised, no, we have just been turned away from Berghain.

What's next jumps around in my memory like chewed-up VHS tape. Somebody knows another club. We're in a taxi. Roads whizz by outside in an unfamiliar blur. We're walking into a building. I remember the building having one floor and set back off a tree-lined straße. I remember handing over change to somebody on a door. Then, as recollections jump about and rush before gradually smoothing out, I'm dancing. I could describe the interior, a musty smell like a church, or the physical dimensions, similar to a community hall where plastic chairs were shoved to the side and the DJs played across from a school assembly style stage. Then I could describe moments, smiles, synchronicities in movement. Feeling energy subtly shift in the crossfade like a breeze through a window. But this wasn't what I took away.

What I found on the dancefloor that night stayed with me over the next month in Maya's apartment. It hovered around in people I met, as I wrote in cafes, walked across the town, road the U-Bahn, stood naked in the cold Spree air after the heat of an *Aufguss* ceremony, had late-night discussions with new friends where politics and art took centre stage. I never felt I had to tone down that dreaded cliche: I'm an artist. And nobody ever spoke about money unless it was to complain about how something had become more expensive. For the next six years, every time I could afford to go on holiday, I'd come back. Clubs would not be the reason I'd eventually move to Berlin, and over time, my frequency of visiting dance spaces became more erratic. I came for the community, the creativity, of being accepted as an outsider and accepting outsiderness in others, and I tuned into sounds that echoed my experiences in the city: echoes of the desolate recent past in Kreuzberg and Schöneberg, deep global rhythms. Drones and noise humming across independent spaces in Neukölln. The international bustle of Mitte and Friedrichshain. Ghettoblasters ridden across the runways of Tempelhofer Airfield. And the passing ambiences of city life.

I didn't own a smartphone back in 2012. Walking home without maps, as sunlight rose over unfamiliar buildings, I never did find out the name of that club or where it was. And what's more, I've never wanted to.

2.

AN ECHO IN THE RUINS

MARK REEDER. SCHÖNEBERG. JOY DIVISION. GENIALE DILLETANTEN. TANGERINE DREAM.

A cold night in Schöneberg, 1979. Gaslit streetlamps flicker shadows over old tenement buildings, some of which have remained in ruin for over thirty years. Within this drizzly sepia, a lone car approaches an address. Inside the vehicle, a hitcher, a young man driven by curiosity. Everywhere he's gone, people have scratched their heads and asked him, why Berlin? From Hamburg to Munich, people have wondered: why would you want to step foot anywhere near this ugly, walled-in city, where the air is cold and the sky is thick with the smokebelch of coal?

The hitcher is reminded by sophisticates, anarchists and anyone with an opinion from Cologne to Düsseldorf that Berlin is no longer the capital. That, divided in two, Berlin is a discarded ruin left over from a time nobody wants to mention, one hundred kilometres into the communist east. And West Berlin, a forgotten outpost way behind enemy lines, reachable on land only via a single, long strip of road ominously nicknamed the Iron Corridor. Along this route, earlier that day, he recounts how the car radio transmitted indecipherable fragments of voices, not too dissimilar from the experimental tape cut-ups of Musique concrète, but in reality, far more likely to be coded transmissions meant for passing covert information. This is the height of the Cold War, after all. Radio-activity as the car courses beyond the Western world, into ruins and the unknown.

There is nothing in West Berlin except cold weather and coal skies – lips tut above their satin lapels in Munich, shiny and libidinous and home to Giorgio Moroder, the king of arpeggiated disco, 'I Feel Love' and sophisticated sex on the dancefloor. Yes, it's true that even if the West German government hadn't gone and waived military conscription to any young German man willing to move to Berlin, why, still, would anyone want to go to West Berlin?

They ask this in Düsseldorf too: a region whose solid industrial backbone has benefited immensely from the Wirtschaftswunder, the upturn, also known as the Miracle on the Rhine, also known in the English language as the Economic Miracle that unexpectedly made West Germany a prosperous global contender following its reconstruction after that thing that nobody mentions. These, incidentally, are the circumstances around which two sons of wealthy Dusseldörfians, Ralf Hütter and Florian Schneider, create, through Kraftwerk. This electronic future echoes and will, over time, far supersede the optimism of a monorail in a world trade fair. The Economic Miracle, he gets told, does not reach West Berlin.

Wherever the hitcher travels, music guides his curiosity. Exotic, hard to locate sounds, travel guides in the form of vinyl long players have led him to West Germany and now leave a trail of sonic breadcrumbs region to region. Otherworldly music: Can in Cologne, Faust and Cluster in Niedersachsen, Neu! in Düsseldorf, Amon Düül and Popol Vuh in Munich. Music that despite the disparate tools used, from tape experiments and electronically generated sounds to guitars and drums, and regardless of the even more disparate operators of these tools spread across a nation, are somehow connected through a desire to start from scratch and walk into the unfamiliar.

And now, this quest has led him to this walled-in, broken city that nobody has a good word to say about, and that there is absolutely, as he gets told and told and told, no economic miracle. His hometown friends in the band Joy Division have heard these sounds too. You can hear touches of this influence in their music: repetitive motorik beats, a droning expansiveness unusual to drab punk Britain. So has another band from his city, The Fall, who, several years later, will play a most affectionate homage to Can and their improvisatory, street-busking singer Damo Suzuki with the apocalyptic psychedelia of 'I Am Damo Suzuki'. Music has been calling him here since the hitcher's first trip to West Germany in 1976. If an Ash Ra Temple album was so hard to get hold of in England, imagine what else there is here lurking in the shadows of a record shop. And when it comes to West Berlin, the fact that not one person is encouraged to come here has made him curious.

Into the gaslamps and drizzle. The car stops, and the hitcher, who, despite the miles travelled and the vinyl discovered, is still a lanky and unfilled-out youth, steps out and walks up the steps to Winterfeldstraße 24. Mark Reeder had spent the better part of his time around records, thumbing through the vinyl in Manchester's Virgin Records so frequently that it only seemed logical, when the vacancy arose, to give the kid a job. In the UK, punk had happened; the older staff, lost in their beards mainlining Little Feet, didn't know their Buzzcocks from their X-Ray Spex and they didn't want to either. This was a time when Robert Plant would use *Melody Maker* to attack punk – it's not musical, they can't play their instruments, says the Led Zeppelin frontman, possibly from the band's private jet.

The older guard in Virgin Records agreed with Plant and it wasn't long before they quit the shop. But Mark Reeder was there. In the evenings, he might have been playing in The Frantic Elevators, a band he formed with the young Mick Hucknall, but in the day, there he was, behind the counter in Lever Street dispensing vinyl. If you wanted something special, something the press hadn't even cottoned on to, go and see Mark. Tony Wilson knew this. Tony Wilson of Factory Records, the Tony Wilson who drew his own blood to sign Joy Division. The Tony Wilson who believed in Happy Mondays when everyone else thought they were a shambles. The Tony Wilson of the Haçienda, the Tony Wilson off the TV. Yes, that Tony Wilson. Tony Wilson would pop by the shop deliberately late on a Saturday after everyone left, avoiding the gazes of people thinking, hey, that's Tony Wilson, and he'd ask young Mark to put by the records that he thought were good. Not the records that the press thought were good, nor the records that were getting the attention, but the records Mark thought were good. Yes, punk may have represented a musical year zero in the UK for the young, bored and disenfranchised, but for the more adventurous new guard, like Wilson, like Joy Division, like The Fall and like Mark Reeder, punk was never a cul-de-sac, and right now, exotic music from Europe is calling him.

'Berlin was so far away back then, beyond the Western world,' Mark says, looking up at the five floors of Winterfeldstraße 24. It's a hot day in July over forty years after that drizzly night he arrived here for that first time. 'It was in the middle of East Germany, you had to go through this transit route. Flying was never an option because it cost something like £650 with British Airways. So people just didn't do it; it was just so far away.' But this wasn't the only thing. The West German boomers who dug music and progress and who, like all those other kids in Western Europe and America, just grew, looked and sounded different from their parents, avoided talk of the war. Instead, opting for a start-everything-from-scratch approach buoyed by the Economic Miracle and reflected in unconventional sounds. But in England, people still certainly were talking about the war. Jokes about humourless Germans on holiday laying out their beach towels with a fanatic precision. Sausages and goosesteps. Two world wars and one world cup. Basil Fawlty doing a Nazi walk. Maybe it takes the curiosity of a wide-eyed kid from the industrial north to take a different attitude. 'Initially, I just thought in coming here I can probably get some of these German imports that you can't get in the UK. I hadn't planned on staying,' Mark laughs. 'I only came to Berlin to buy some records, and I never left.'

We're stood on the doorstep of Winterfeldstraße 24. The house belonged to the driver who picked him up that day. A stroke of luck: during the ride, Mark revealed he had nowhere to stay. Well, you can stay at our house, the driver says. Apart from some students living on the second floor, the place is empty, the driver tells him, it's about to be demolished. He remembers the green door, still green, and beyond that, how grand and unusual it was to have marble flooring. 'He said I can stay for as long as I like until it gets torn down.' The man gave Mark a skeleton key to his own six-room flat, way up on the fifth floor. Parquet floorboards, white marble bathroom, stuck on the deck. No paperwork, no questions and no one cares,' Mark says. 'The whole house had electricity and gas. In England, they turn everything off, whereas here they didn't give a shit, and this beautiful old house which was about to be torn down to build a new block of flats, this rat-infested place with its outside toilet, they were going to tear it down. They never did.'

Looking up from outside, I could subjectively claim Winterfeldstraße 24 is by far the prettiest house on the straße right now. Green and healthy plant boxes drip down from where they've freshly been watered onto the ground below. A common symptom of summer here, as you walk around, you might well receive a drip, sometimes more onto your shoulder, your hair, your bag. Balconies hang directly over the paving and nobody seems to look down when they're watering. The whole tenement building resembles a wedding cake, not like the grand Stalinist style of architecture found a few kilometres east along Karl-Marx-Allee, with its bold and intricately detailed buildings that get commonly called to mind as prime wedding cake. Rather, Winterfeldstraße 24's layers of tenement yellow stuck and red bricks glisten with a maintained love that in today's July sunlight could be icing sugar. Subjectively, of course, and in comparison, the surrounding vista feels dry, functional.

Even the cafe on the corner, whose sign boasts of serving 'more than a breakfast' but feels, as the same with music, when something sets out to make the most amount of tastes happy, a bit flavourless. That is, except opposite. Here, most of the straße is taken up by one building. On the night he arrived, this vast building reminds Mark of home, and with its Coronation Street terrace-style bricks, it's easy to see why. But this is the Fernmeldeamt. A survivor of the Weimar era, survivor of Allied bombs, survivor of Nazi occupation and survivor of Cold War-era American occupation too. Like so many buildings in this torn-apart stadt, opposing sides have, at different points in history, occupied its space. The Fernmeldeamt is still the largest telephone exchange in Europe. I think of Mark's journey here, traversing along the Iron Corridor, the radio transmitting those broken fragments of voice, code, distant bleeps. I wonder, behind the Yorkshire brick, down pine-wooden corridors, along wires plugging in and pulled out of modular switchboards and intercepted by operators who most likely live in Schöneberg, working in shifts and having a drink after just across the platz in the bar called Slumberland, did these signals travel through here? Were they benign code, or am I letting my Cold War imagination run riot? Now, the vast, factory-length struc-ture is occupied by Telekom, owners of the subsidised yet actually credible online electronic music magazine, *Telekom Electronic Beats*.

'You look like you've just come from an early morning duel,' Mark jokes. The tightness of my FFP2 mask has left what he calls a *schnitt*, a nick along a cheek. He removes his mask so that I can take a photo of him on the steps of Winterfeldstraße 24. He wears his mask everywhere on the streets, only taking it off as we sit on chairs at scorching hot cafe terraces. He's wearing black. Black short-sleeved shirt, black trousers, black Ray-Bans. A uniform of sorts, but not of the kind that has become a trademark – old militia jackets, Soviet officer suits, historic uniforms of authority that he somehow manages to wear in a way far more the dandy than military nut. Now in his early sixties, hair white and a little thinning yet still as precisely in place as it was when he brought Joy Division over for their only concert here at the Kant Kino on 21 January 1980. Mark's life in Berlin, and his role in the development of music culture here, which along the way, despite producing the very last record in the GDR, got him labelled as a *Subversiv-Dekadent* by the Stasi, would adhere to mythical status if it wasn't for the fact that he's so damn approachable. Pre-pandemic, on occasion, I'd bump into him in a cafe and he'd always low-key radiate Northern ease. A friend of mine once lived in a shared commune next door to him, and one Christmas, the commune invited all of their neighbours over for festive lunch. My friend recollects how, as potatoes were being served, wine bottles uncorked and the air was a little awkward, as you can imagine, maintaining a room of disparate strangers, gradually whispers went around that the gentleman with the in-place industrial hair, spooning gravy onto his plate whilst politely ignoring the boisterous singing of another neighbour, is actually, well, kind of a legend. A Berliner for over forty years, yet a Lancashireman since ever.

'Nearly all the people who used to live in the seventies and early eighties in Schöneberg,' he tells me as we leave the house and head into the now chi-chi grid of cafes, boutiques and kitas that used to, back in the day, be his *kiez*. 'Nearly all of them still live here, and in the meantime, they've stopped being students and become business people or whatever. If you fight for a house, and you put a lot of work into maintaining it, keeping it and stopping it from being torn down or being turned into luxury apartments, you tend to want to hang on to that.'

During the eighties, as the one or two hundred people that made up West Berlin's underground nightlife swirled and drank their way across clubs and bars in Schöneberg and Kreuzberg and everyone played in everyone's bands, Mark had his synth-pop duo Die Unbekannten. Die Unbekannten morphed into Shark Vegas, who released one of the most sought-after Factory 12" singles, 'You Hurt Me'. Of course, even if the tune didn't evoke a melancholic electro swagger like that of his friends New Order, it only feels natural that the man who acted as Tony Wilson's record consultant those Friday evenings back in Manchester's Virgin Records should eventually be rewarded with having his very own Factory serial number: FAC111. But Mark wasn't just a scenester; Mark was a smuggler. Smuggling cassettes across the Iron Curtain to the punk-deprived kids in the east. Smuggling cassettes because when you're going through a gap in a wall between two opposing realities, through the military scrutiny at Checkpoint Charlie, 12" vinyl is impossible to conceal. Eventually, he'd smuggle across an actual band, Die Toten Hosen, for whom he was the sound engineer, organising highly illegal punk gigs in churches in East Berlin, the first time western people had done this. Much, much later, after the Wall fell and the two sides of the city learnt to connect again through ecstasy, techno and abandoned spaces, Mark was managing a young East German DJ he'd discovered called Paul Van Dyk and extolling the virtues of a different variation of warehouse-filling dance music called trance. He set up a label. The label he named MFS, the initials taken from the East German Ministry For State Security, the Stasi, those same shady operatives who'd labelled him *Subversiv-Dekadent*. Except now, MFS stood for Masterminded For Success.

Yet still, we're getting way ahead of ourselves. In 1979, when Mark arrived, he says there wasn't a scene: 'Berlin wasn't seen as a musical city, it was always viewed as a political place. This was where the third world war would definitely happen, east meets west, all that rubbish. When Bowie came to Berlin, he obviously put the city on the musical map, but still, people weren't lining up to come here. He made *Heroes* and then left ,and then there was a gap, there was nothing for a couple of years, until the dawn of the eighties, really.' At the end of Winterfeldstraße, we reach a secluded platz set off the road, where benches are spaced neatly around a cleared space of yellow pebbles, like a Japanese garden. It's calm and peaceful and I can imagine it being a good spot for a pensioner to let their dog have a quick sniff around. We stand on tiny pebbles and Mark tells me this used to be the site of a bar named die Ruine. 'It was just the rest of what was left after a bomb attack,' Mark says, 'the owners thought: this room is still intact, let's turn what's left into a bar. Back then, there were no rules and regulations; you could find a space and open it up twenty-four hours a day.'

'There was a big gap compared to the UK,' Mark says. It must have been strange, I ask him, leaving Manchester, a place with such a vibrant musical culture, one that he himself was already so connected into the mechanisms of. 'People in Manchester made music so they could get away, so they could escape. Boredom, no prospects, no future, that was it for most kids. I was really privileged. I had a job, nearly all my friends had no job, and no idea what they could do with their lives, signing on, that was it. If you didn't go to university your life was going to be on the dole, and no one gave you any form of encouragement. Punk rock gave people that encouragement; you can get a guitar for ten quid on your dole money.' Yet, this is the context in which Robert Plant used *Melody Maker* to condemn punk. 'It was such a disgraceful thing to say,' Mark tells me. 'I didn't listen to Led Zeppelin for decades after that.'

Instead, Mark finds himself as a newcomer in a city where, in his first couple of years here, if there was a scene, it must have felt hidden away. 'Buzzcocks had played here and Sex Pistols were supposed to and then they didn't. In Germany, punk was looked upon as being something a bit suspicious. Travelling around the rest of Germany, Düsseldorf? Yeah, maybe, but Munich? They'd never even heard of the Sex Pistols, so something like Joy Division didn't even enter into it. When I got here, punk was just starting to emerge. They had one punk rock band with one single, Tempo.' Tempo were from Schöneberg, their debut EP, released in 1979, begins with the aptly named 'Waiting For The Eighties'. It's a fun jaunt, veering towards the new wave power-pop of a 'My Sharona', like the music over a montage sequence in an eighties teen comedy. Yet, in its sentiment, I picture the song soundtracking something just around the corner, needing to happen. The lyrics are all no sleep and no rest and waiting for the eighties and their neon bars and classic cars. Weirdly prophetic. He mentions another band too, called PVC, who'd already supported Iggy Pop and who called their music Wall City Rock. Music indeed from a walled-in city.

Punk may not have developed into a vibrant scene when Mark arrived. Still, sounds were being made here that somehow captured the ruined buildings and decaying streets just as vividly as the way Joy Division transmitted the ennui of youth in the industrial north of England. Tangerine Dream, one of the sonic breadcrumbs dotted around West Germany who had drawn Mark's curiosity, were from Schöneberg. Sonically, they drew from a pallet utterly contrasting to punk: beat-less and instrumental, electronic and atmospheric, *Kosmische* music made without a roadmap that, particularly on the 1975 album *Rubycon*, that actually made a commercial impression in the UK. 'I remember I was really excited when I heard Tangerine Dream had a new album coming out,' he says, 'and when we played *Rubycon* in the Virgin Records shop through the loudspeakers, it sounded unlike anything else at the time.'

The music on *Rubycon* was made up of two seventeen-minute long tracks where textures, gurgles, arpeggiations, moments of melody and synthetic choral sounds seem to emerge out of ancient shadows. 'I thought it sounded dark and mysterious and somehow primeval,' Mark says. Whereas those other electronic pioneers, Kraftwerk, were celebrating newness and technology like champagne-popping industrialists, the music on *Rubycon* could have been made in a damp cave. 'Actually, I was doing quite a bit of potholing and hiking at the time,' Mark says, thinking back to his surroundings pre-Berlin. 'And when I heard this album, my thoughts were transported to this barren landscape – it still does. I played this album every day, non-stop for weeks on end.' Tangerine Dream captured the mid-seventies in Schöneberg. Hippie-esque yet brutally grey. Long reverbs like empty streets.

The harmonics of 1979 Schöneberg, echoes and ruins, strolling in his new *kiez*, the sound of wrecking balls of Kufurstenstraße, sharing a nod with the prostitutes who've already noted him as an uninterested local. Maybe they'll get trade from businessmen checking into one of the only nearby hotels, Hotel Berlin Berlin. Then, there's the harmonics of a new language, an umlaut hanging above a vowel. The *eszett*, that sharp S sound that, written down, looks a little like a B. All unfamiliar muscles in an English person's mouth. 'I had a Collins phrasebook, but it didn't get more complex than *Wo ist der banhoff?*, stuff like that,' he laughs. 'I didn't have anything other than talking to people, but I refused to speak English to anyone. If I want to be here then I want to know what makes Germans tick, what drove a nation into following Hitler; they willingly followed this person. I was like, maybe it's part of the make-up of Germans, but most Germans didn't want to know what their parents were in the war and they found me weird because I talked about it.' And language was key. 'I was also curious about Germans supposedly not having a sense of humour; they must have. I discovered Karl Valentine, the comedian, he was hilarious; *Berliner Ballade* with Gert Fröbe, filmed after the war, he lives in a ruin like we lived in a ruin and it's hilarious. I thought, if I don't learn German, I'll never understand these fine nuances and how Germans tick.'

Meanwhile, as Mark is settling in, Rob Gretton from back in Manchester gets in contact. Mark knew him before he became the manager of Joy Division. Mark knew Ian Curtis before then too, because working in a record shop you meet all these kinds of people. *An Ideal For Living*, the band's first EP, was being re-released as a 12". 'Rob was like, can you maybe give a few copies to radio stations in Berlin? Because there are British soldiers posted here.' Rob had the idea that this would help sell a few in Germany, and maybe it'd get played on the radio. Did it work? 'Nah, forget it, it didn't work. Rob sent me a big box of records, and I sent them to all these magazines, the magazines of the day that were available in Germany; they were trash, really. No chance. Of course, I believed in this record wholeheartedly; this was the best band in the entire universe. There was no other band, even in Manchester, like Joy Division. I thought, "People have to understand it; they'll love it when they hear it."' But I'm taking it that they didn't? 'No, they didn't. No one was interested, not in the slightest. Back then, it was considered unlistenable, you know, like, what's this rubbish?'

An Ideal For Living might have become landfill, but what he did have from Manchester, stowed away with him, waiting for

Mark to pluck up the courage to use it, was a local address. 'I have no idea how I got this address. Working at Virgin Records, you pick up all sorts of stuff,' he tells me. Edgar Froese, the enigmatic, sometimes described as difficult, figurehead of Tangerine Dream. 'I realised that he lived quite close. So maybe after six weeks, I decided, "Right, now go and have a look, see if I can say hello." I went round to his house, rang the doorbell and his wife answered the door, this kid was hanging on her leg, and she goes, "Yes?" I go, "Is Edgar Froese here?" She's like, "Who are you?" I'm like, "Oh, I'm from Manchester." She says, "He's not here, he's on tour in England."'

Emptiness creates echo. Bodies and material dry this up. The desolation of Tangerine Dream's Schöneberg that fed strange reverbs and beautiful longing harmonics are soaked into the skin and garments of leisurely crowds along Goltzstraße. Dried out in the bustle of lunchtime meal offers, the ghostly whistle of forgotten synth textures trodden into paving cracks along the way by ageing tourists now fanning themselves below bistro awnings. The only reverb is from the heat radiating off the paving and we're parched.

'Most of the cafes at the time around here were hippie haunts; you'd get your *milchkaffee* in a bowl without a handle and the walls would be plastered with posters and stickers of visiting hippie bands.' Mark suggests we go to Café M. Maybe Goltzstraße has, over the years, slinked off the barren hippie fug and swooned into a late-middle-aged respectability. Maybe any whispers of the wilderness of Tangerine Dream's *Rubycon* exist only in the memories of its older inhabitants. Still, its musical past is proudly lit in the zigzagging letter M that hangs above the front of Café M. It's a neon red M from another time, fertile and futuristic, zigzagging like a waveform.

In the seventies, Bowie and Iggy were regulars. Once, a couple of years back, maybe through sentiment or maybe through vicarious inhalation, I came here on the anniversary of Bowie's departure. That night, there were Bowie pilgrims, there were older locals that I like to imagine knew him, and there were some, like me, who didn't exactly know why they were here. Photos of David and Iggy, *Lust For Life* era, hang in the toilets the way an Italian restaurant might display a photo of Al Pacino with a spoonful of linguini. Photos reminding you as you pee who Café M's famous clientele were. But it was in the eighties when Café M became a haunt for a community of like-minded artists, musicians, anarchists, hellraisers, art school kids and film students, and, of course, Mark. The *Geniale Dilletanten*. Deliberately misspelt.

At any point in the night, here in Café M, or a stroll away along Kurfurstendamm upstairs in Café Einstein, over in Dschungel or across into Koti at S036. There are other places, of course. It is in these hours and in these places that much of the footage of the film *B-Movie: Lust And Sound In West Berlin 1979–1989* takes place. Assembled by Jörg A. Hoppe, Klaus Maeck and Heiko Lange, the entire film is both an essay and a montage, woven through Super 8 footage of late-night excess, afternoons huddled in cafes, music experimentation in shops, and taking the starring role is Mark: witness, participant, catalyst. It is effectively the story, through Mark's narration, of Berlin's underground arts subculture in the eighties. There is a scene where two conspirators are seen nestled up along a bar, both agents of the *Geniale Dilletante*. One, Blixa Bargeld, sings over the sound of industrial destruction in the band Einstürzende Neubauten. The other is the Australian polymath Nick Cave, who has left his band The Birthday Party and for the next two years has made Berlin his home. The two have become conspiratorially close, they look wrecked and they, says Mark's narration, 'are waging a war against sleep'.

Out all night, every night. I tell Mark that I've been told that people went out so much in the 1980s to escape the cold because the coal heating would take so long to heat the flats up. 'That's a lie,' Mark interjects with the bluster of a best man at a wedding who's remembered the punchline. 'They've lied to you, it's not because the coal heating didn't heat the flats up warm enough, it's because they couldn't get up in time to go to the coal merchant to buy the coal to heat the flats in the first place.' We see Café M's terrace tables and chairs, all the same primary red, Suspiria red, laid out on the street ahead. 'That's the reality; they went out all night and slept all day. And then you'd get up at ten to six and you'd realise, crap, I've missed the coal merchant, he's going to be shut in two minutes, so you'd have to go out again.'

Those early evenings, keeping warm, Mark might choose to head over to the Arsenal Kino on Fuggerstraße, 'which was always a real haunt. You'd see all these Tarkovsky films and all the avant-garde stuff and it'd start really early, like seven o'clock. You'd spend a couple of hours in the cinema, keeping nice and warm watching movies. And then you'd move on to a cafe, hang around there for a while, then the bar, and then the club, and then it was the next day and time to go home.' Except today we don't get into Café M because it's not open yet. We see a sign saying that the bar opens at 4pm. Back then, 4pm would have been an early morning. There's a tinge of something in Mark's reaction, like he's missed a small beat.

We do a circuit, up to Nollendorfplatz then, grabbing a quick stop for refreshments before heading along back to Winterfeldplatz. Mark points to a long bar, closed with tinted windows and with a blue boat-wood deck called Slumber Land. 'This was the original Dschungel,' he says like it's an afterthought, which I guess maybe it is. In the 1980s, *Dschungel*, German for Jungle, would emigrate out of the boat-blue awnings here and manifest nearby into its own twilight world where the reality of Schöneberg was kept as far away as possible. A safe space where people who'd forgotten to buy coal and, consequently, as you do when you've forgotten to buy coal and have to go out all night again, might include the actress and singer Zazie de Paris, the designer Claudia Skoda, Mark, of course, Gudrun Gut, Christiane F. and without doubt Nick Cave and Blixa Bargeld, possibly still conspiring against sleep. But along here, where we're stood now, the Jungle in Winterfeldplatz remained firmly in the echoes and ruins.

'It used to be a kindergarten,' Mark tells me. 'They'd gone and just left paintings on the wall of *The Jungle Book* film. It was a very hippie place like everything else in Schöneberg, deck-chairs, Steve Hillage on the stereo, but when the couple that ran it split up, the girl decided she was going to do something else, so she went to Nurnberger Straße, twenty minutes' walk away and opened a new place, more new wavey fashionable, still called The Jungle, still maintaining the name.' Without

Mowgli and Baloo peering down on you, the new Jungle used blinds to shut out the world. Plus, with a notoriously hard to get in door policy, I ask Mark if I'm being glib by making the comparison of Jungle to Studio54. 'That was the kind of image they wanted to create, to have our own place exclusively for people in the know; you couldn't just get in.'

Romy Haag, the cabaret performer who had a romantic relationship with Bowie. David Hemmings, who directed Bowie in the forgotten, Berlin-set *Just A Gigolo*, starring alongside another Schöneberg native, Marlene Dietrich, regulars. Mick Jagger, Grace Jones and Barbra Streisand, regulars when in town. 'It was a bit like Berghain really: we don't want idiots, we want people who are nice, who fit in, who are part of our scene, and even if we don't know them because they've just arrived, you can tell immediately if they belong. It's not just because they decide to wear a black T-shirt, there are other things, there's other chemistry.' Thinking of Berghain, I remember the first time I finally got inside and feeling like I'd been accepted into a secret world. 'That's what the Jungle represented; if you were doing music, films or writing, you could go to the Jungle and have a like-minded conversation or dance.'

I think of the Berlin I know myself, international, progressive but a budget airline away. The night before I meet Mark, I'm with a friend drinking Flensburger in Laidak, a cafe that stays open late at night on the corner of Mainzer Straße and Boddinstraße in Neukölln. Here, smoke fills across the ripped leather sofas and the upholstery is covered in tags and graffiti: Gegen Nazis, Stoppt Die AFD, defiantly left-wing, nobody cares about money or at least everyone is extremely careful to project that they don't care about money. Amongst the many shades of gender, loose-vested and shaven-headed girls and mullet-haired boys with painted nails drink and smoke, read books and chat. It stays open until the staff decide they can't be bothered to serve anymore and stack the chairs. I hear punk music led by out-of-tune German singing being played out of an old Acer PC, its cracked screen perched by the cash register. We could all be the children of the *Geniale Dilletanten*, I wonder, living through a forty-year-plus echo that has grown out the ruins.

'I'm not nostalgic; it's part of my life and part of my history, I suppose, but I don't dwell on it,' Mark says as we get close to Nollendorfplatz U-Bahn. 'There are things I miss, the thrill of going into East Berlin, of smuggling stuff across the border.' We go into the station, the thick air of ancient cigarettes embedded into the station's plaster. It's a strange feeling knowing that we're about to follow a route that no longer exists.

3.

ACCELERATING, OUT OF THE PAUSE

DJ FUCKOFF. NEUKÖLLN. PRENZLAUER BERG. SAFE SPACE. THE PAUSE

'Terminator!' A deep voice cuts through the transience of Alexanderplatz U-Bahn station.

'Terminator!' I hear again. I look along the platform and see a man who I guess is in his fifties, grinning from underneath a red baseball cap, arms leaned out across a bench. His voice is a ripped staccato that echoes along the track like a sample from the nineties.

'Hey, Terminator!' The man is in no hurry for the upcoming U2 to Pankow. I realise he's trying to attract the attention of a young guy, walking with rigid stealth along the platform, deeply insulated inside the most silver of silver jackets.

'Hey you, Terminator!' The man isn't giving up yet. 'Did you see the last one?' None of this is breaking the silver jacketed man's stride. Which, I've clocked, does have an intense T-1000-like determination.

'Well, that was pretty hot!' says the man, reaching a saxophone out of his lap. He puts it to his lips and blows. Long, sonorous notes that could be *The Terminator* theme music reverberate like an introduction to the approaching train. The train slows. Those whirrs and long beeps the yellow carriages make as they grind to a halt merge into the saxophone. I jump on, move into the carriage, find a handrail. Filtered, much of the top end removed but I can still hear sax. The doors close. The carriage makes another of its little coos and sighs, this time a horn, a piped and warped electronic horn. For a second, as we pull away, the man and the carriage play together: cacophonous, in and out of harmony, just another overlapping layer in a dense city. Speeding off, through the windows I see him one last moment, his long tracksuited legs leaning forward. I notice coins scattered sparsely across the velvet interior of an open saxophone case by his feet.

In Berlin, there are places where the U-Bahn will raise itself out of the subway. Where the carriage you're riding on will arch out of a dark subterranean tunnel and snake its yellow metallic body across the raised viaduct. When it does this, like where I am today on the U2, the carriages blur you past the third floor of tenement buildings, shrinking scrubs of wasteland, dwindling undeveloped spaces. I become the passenger of my own nostalgia; moments come whizzing by. Moments like an unsteady sip from a Staro shared with a Tinder date, laughing as the beer froths out onto the carriage floor as we rattle along above Möckernbrücke, the black depths of the canal below. Another. The U3 heading towards Schlesi, sharing a rolled-up cigarette with a stranger above the curve across that Burger Meister kiosk. And here where I am now, drawing to a halt in Eberswalde Straße, up north in Prenzlauer Berg. Once anything but chi-chi, perhaps if anywhere, it's Prenzlauer Berg that has seen the most drastic change of any part of Berlin over the last thirty years. Where I'm jumping into is Tribeca, is Highbury and Islington, but to view this swan solely on high rents and costly boutiques neglects a radical and recent past. Still, it's far from the most obvious place I'd expect to meet with DJ Fuckoff.

'When I move, people are definitely going to tell I come from Neukölln,' Zoe had said the last time we met, her pink manicures glistening in the sun as she drank from a mug of *Heiße Schokolade*, 'I'm moulded into the scenery here.' This last time was months earlier and she was still living in Neukölln, as was I. It was mid-summer and we sat on a bench outside the Leutchstoffe, a cafe deep in the heart of Neukölln that sits parallel to a ravine where the loop of the ring train passes deep below. The staff are super friendly, young. In the bathroom, there are free tampons in a pasta jar and a tag above the door reads *Klein Platz für AFD*. No Place For AFD: the far-right political party. *Antifaschismus*. From an angle like this, at least, Neukölln feels raw and inclusive. Even after a decade-plus of absorbing the overspill of gentrification from Kreuzberg, Neukölln takes on the appearance of a kind of last stand. If something progressive is happening, and if it's to have any kind of swell to it, it'll most likely be somewhere here south of the canal.

It was July and Zoe was just beginning to travel as DJ Fuckoff. Sets in Hamburg and Kyiv and Warsaw that month and then back home to the apartment she was living in at the time, just down the hill off noisy, chaotic Karl-Marx Straße.

Before the pandemic, she'd barely played out in Berlin. In her live sets on streaming platform Hör Radio, during and just after the first lockdown, I recognised the flux of influences and values of the Neukölln I lived in. She did indeed feel moulded into the scenery. Then, as we were sat that day, she told me she was moving to Prenzlauer Berg.

'Maybe I change my name to something polite and have USBs hanging off my Louis Vuitton,' she laughed. We both have quite loud voices. 'I could open a children's clothing store. All the sexual tension has been released. DJ Fuckoff is over.' The sexual tension she refers to is at the core of her sound, where elements of techno, happy hardcore, psy-trance, juke and breakbeat are galvanised through an R&B swagger and upfrontness towards sexuality. In '(B.I.M.B) Bills In My Booty', posted on SoundCloud that week in July, she raps: 'I want 50,000 dollar bills in my booty/hold the phone/All you boys trynna taste this pussy/whatchoo want?' Or then there's the robotised mantra of 'Lick It': 'Lick it/Suck it/Feel it then just fuck it.'

She works at a breakneck speed on productions, during one recording session Ableton-ing through ten to twenty ideas, spanning tempos, working through trance to techno to chill before she lands on the idea that she'll climb into. 'I think it's my ADHD brain,' she says. 'I can't settle on one thing. And then the last idea is the idea that I stick with but then even within the track itself, I will create different tracks.' She asks me if this is the same kind of process I go through with writing. I say I can't speak for anyone else but, for me, yes, sometimes. We both agree that the ideas you don't end up pursuing have the same appeal as someone you don't want to talk to at a party.

Throughout this conversation we had in the summer, little jokes about her moving to Prenzlauer Berg kept creeping in. About gentrification. About Saturday markets and boutiques. Posh prams and hemp yoga mats. If this sounds catty, and I'm not saying that it doesn't, it's worth remembering that Berliners can be incredibly territorial. We fight for our little *islas* and making jokes about other districts is a form of unity in a city where, aside from each little *kiez* having its own distinct flavour, the disparity between the narrative of Berlin as an endless playground of abandoned buildings and low rent, a narrative now upsold to international investment, and the reality that this is a population exploited by landlords, where rent prices have increased 70% within a decade and where accommodation is hard to come by, ripples into our bones. So that when you do find a home where it just feels right, where your neighbours are your kind of people, where the guys in the *Späti* are super sweet and you can just effortlessly slip on your shoes to pop out, not only do you want to stay put, but you've fought bureaucracy, the odds and claimed your little Berlin perch. Subsequently, jokes arise. Neuköllners make jokes about bouji Prenzlauerbergians, Prenzlauerbergians make jokes about black-clad partygoing Neuköllners. And so forth.

But that was in the summer, and a humid July afternoon has now become a brisk November lunchtime. We're meeting today at Bonanza Coffee Heroes on Oderberger Straße. I leave the U-Bahn and walk the steps down to the exit onto the straße, passing a group of school children eating Risa Chicken out of paper wrappers. The smell of fried chicken, then the smell of donuts, then the smell of just pure cold air. It runs fresh along this wide straße. Thirty years ago, it would have been thick with the heavy fug of coal smoke. This former DDR district was, immediately after the Wall fell and during what became known as The Wonderful Year of Anarchy, a cultural frontline. East really did meet west, in many cases for the first time.

Once, not long after I moved to Berlin, the writer Paul Hockenos met with me. The author of *Berlin Calling*, who as a young American left-wing journalist covering the collapse of communism, arrived into this district where half of the buildings were abandoned, façades on the outside falling down. He told me how Prenzlauer Berg became 'this big bohemian retreat because if you had an idea and a crowbar, you could get into any one of these buildings, more or less, take one of the apartments and then start paying rent on it.' Inside, apartments frequently didn't have bathrooms; toilets were tucked into hall landings and shared with neighbours. During this wonderful year of anarchy, where two cities became one again at a speed far quicker than any kind of legality could keep up with, the police were powerless to intervene and the empty buildings in Prenzlauer Berg created a context where 'East Germans were meeting West Germans for the very first time,' Paul had said, 'and they were getting to know one another in a way that the rest of the country would later in the decade.'

I sat with Paul over an afternoon tea in a restaurant that doubles as a wine shop. The classic American intellectual overseas, he spoke with the twang of a thoughtful mid-seventies

Jack Nicholson, and like the district itself, he's lived through all of the changes and seen that early nineties radicalism soften. As I mentioned earlier, I have a loud voice, and at one point my volume jumped up in excitement at something he said. Paul made the most minimal gesture. A hand on a table, a calm 'If you could lower your . . .', and I realised that we were sitting in his *kiez*. 'Well, you know, Berlin, it's just a big village, and we all get kind of attached to our little parts of that village where we're comfortable,' Paul told me. 'A lot of the former single bohemians of the 1990s ended up meeting other single bohemians of the 1990s and settling down. The bohemians started making babies too, and there's no one neighbourhood in all of Germany where the fertility rate is higher and where there is more concentration of schools and kindergartens than right here in Prenzlauer Berg.' Right now, those kids, the ones with the Risa Chicken crossing onto the U-Bahn, could they be the children of former radicals? Do they have parents that thirty years earlier had forgone bathrooms for living at the very frontline of social reunification? More than anywhere else in the city, the answer would be yes.

I turn left onto Oderberger Straße; Bonanza Coffee Heroes is on one side, and on the other, there's Zoe locking up her bike. She waves and crosses the road. I ask how her weekend went. 'Poland was amazing but the journey back was rough,' she says. Yesterday morning, after de-tangling herself from the afterparty, tired but exhilarated, USBs, overnight bag, cash fee, she makes the train in Krakow, destination Berlin Hauptbahnhof. A menagerie of beats and moments with people she's met over the weekend spinning around her head, some lingering, some disintegrating like smoke, and then somewhere around the Polish–German border her train is grounded. On the tracks, hours pass, the comedown is overtaking, it's real, the comedown express to Hauptbahnhof is grounded and there's no news of when it'll move again. 'I very nearly got out and ordered an Uber; it would have cost me a hundred euros,' she tells me. Immediately it hits me. 'Of course,' I say, 'it's Tuesday.'

Today, Zoe's tucked into a wool hat and gloves; she has no make-up, her vibe is keep it easy and grab a pastry. Since wet met in the summer, her bookings have grown. DJing nearly every weekend, sometimes at parties held within pandemic regulations in Berlin, but also now across Germany, in Cologne, in Hamburg and across Europe. Then, the afterparty, which, she says, she can't resist. 'And suddenly,' she says, 'I'm like, "Hey, catch my train. Gotta go home." And I have a two-day, three-day recovery period.' Which I've just realised we're right in the middle of. As we push open the doors into the warm coffee shop, I suddenly feel guilty that I've dragged her out mid-DJ-hibernation. 'I was asleep till 12:30 and now I actually feel really good,' she says with the breeze of someone living a life of exactly what they've asked the universe for. The travel. The food. The cities. Meeting interesting people and railing across Europe with a memory stick passport and a gift for creating energy. She describes it as an overwhelming happiness. As she travels, there are moments of beauty: the other week, playing in an abandoned sanitarium in the Carpathian Mountains where, behind the DJ booth, a glass window overlooked a forest and she saw the sun rising through the trees. In the castle she stayed in, photographs of the previous owners, their staff, photographs crawling backwards through history. 'But there's been chaotic stuff too.' A dancefloor culture re-emerging from its pause can be clumsy like an underused muscle. Recently, a promoter's friend found the smoke machine. 'He was really trigger happy,' she recalls. 'People in the crowd were choking, and one of the girls was like, "The smoke, it's too much, it's too much, no one in the crowd can breathe." And I fucking looked at the guy and he's just sitting under the booth, smashing on the smoke button and he couldn't see anything, oblivious.'

All of the beauty and all of the chaos each weekend and I'm beginning to understand how the calm of Prenzlauer Berg can be so welcome. 'Oh my God, I really love it,' Zoe says as we take seats along the roadside. 'I love Neukölln but I didn't realise how much I needed a change, just to be somewhere more quiet. Living on Karl-Marx-Straße, as I was for most of my time since arriving in Berlin, it's not really possible. I would get off the train and then it's straight into all this lalalala noise. Also . . .' – she pauses and leans in – 'I realise that I'm wearing black all the time now and I never wore black before Berlin. Ever. I was wearing lots of colourful shit: really bright reds and yellows and greens.' It's at this moment it occurs to me, from conversations we've had where Zoe's spoken about her parents, about how in infancy she grew up around psy-trance and then, even in that moment that sparked those first thoughts about coming to Berlin, which could be traced back to one night dancing on a beach in Goa, could it be that aside from the clothing, the bling and the hustle, that underneath it all, she's a hippy a heart? 'I was a bit hippy. My parents, they were hippies, but a bit bogan too, you know this word, right?' Zoe says.

I know a tiny bit about bogan culture through hand-me-down jokes about uncouthness. Born in the late nineties in Auckland, New Zealand, at a time when trance was travelling around the world and white labels were landing into the underground party scene that existed outside of Auckland's mainstream club culture. 'My dad was doing psy-trance parties,' she tells me. 'They had this acid hippie free-thinking vibe. They stopped doing drugs when they had me and my sister but they let me think whatever I wanted to think and dress however I wanted to dress and do whatever I wanted to do. My mum would say, "Hey, if you're in trouble, you can talk to me but go figure out the world."'

'I was really young, but my dad had a record store on Karangahape Road. The most famous street in my city for clubs; it was a street where you could feel free and liberated. K Road, they call it.' Post-war, Karangahape Road was the premier street for department stores, cinemas, hairdressers, a glittering promenade, the Kiwi Ku'Damm. After the construction of a motorway in the sixties forced locals to relocate en mass, business declined, the stretch fell into neglect. Over time, subsequent low rents and the wide berth given to it from conservative-minded Aucklanders, leaning into the lexicon of K Road as a red-light district fertilised the conditions for clubs, bars and cafes to open. Hence, bohemian rebirth. 'Everyone was very different there,' Zoe recalls, the steam from our drinks evaporating into cold air. 'I grew up at his record store a lot, walking down the street, there were sex clubs, I saw drag queens who'd hang out, a lot of alternative looking people, a lot of hippies and I realised, okay, not everyone is a conservative farm

New Zealander, which I went to school with.' At school, Zoe struggled to connect with other children. 'No one at school had any kind of exposure to the stuff I did; their parents had completely different jobs, mostly office jobs, they didn't know anything about electronic music and that was my whole world. The other kids would create problems about things that didn't seem important to me. I was like, "Why do you care about that?" It was all lots of drama. I was always thinking, "Hey, these kids are weird, or maybe I'm weird!"'

'When I was eighteen, I was still in high school and I think only maybe three people know this. My mom definitely doesn't know. My sister doesn't know and I guess this also makes sense with my DJ Fuckoff stuff but I started working as a waitress in a strip club. I was doing this without anyone knowing and it was my way of being, "Okay, fuck everyone, fuck everything." I want to explore my own shit, I wanted to see the world and I was so bored with the stuff that my friends were doing in high school, all the drama, and the most extreme thing that I could probably do was go start working in a strip club. It opened me up a lot to what I wanted to do in the coming years, which is now DJ Fuckoff.' Hippie. Bogan. Outsider. She reflects: 'I had to get out of high school to even realise and find the kind of people into the same stuff as me.'

We talked about how she came to Berlin. 'At a psy-trance party, the start of every story,' she laughs. Meeting a guy called Alex on the beach in Goa. Alex was from Berlin. She told him she wanted to DJ. They both conspired. A while later, he released Zoe's hip hop tape on his label; she came for the launch. But it was after a night at the decade-long running sex positive and safe space prioritising Cocktail D'Amour, held that time at Griessmuehle, that she decided she had to live here. 'It was such a beautiful mix of techno, disco and house, people dressing how they want, people not dressing at all if they want. I said this is a place where my energy feels really good, around these people. I felt comfortable. The first few weeks were intense because I was alone. I'd travelled alone before but in terms of saying to myself I'm going to be here for a while, I'm going to settle in. I'd never done this. I was just walking the streets drinking Sterni. I went on a lot of Tinder dates. It's an interesting way to get to know the city. And then I had to find a job because I ran out of money.'

At that moment, from where we're sat on small, wooded tables from the cafe along the side of the straße, the stench of petrol hits our noses and causes a break in our flow. Everyone looks around and at each other. 'Is that a gas leak?' says an elegant young woman lifting the front wheels of her pram onto the paving. 'I guess the good news, though,' I say across to the lady, 'is that if we can smell it, we probably don't have Covid.' Nobody laughs. Zoe sniggers politely. When we met just months earlier in the summer, Zoe's reputation for galvanising bodies was in early ascendence and it coincided with the cautious reopening of dancefloors. DJ Fuckoff is just one of several identities. Zoe makes hip hop under another moniker. Then there's the time recently she found herself writing a sweet love song, finding a romantic side far from the upfront sexuality she projects elsewhere. 'At first, it was just my expression,' she told me. 'And yeah, I wanna talk about dicks, I wanna talk about sex, I wanna talk about whatever the fuck I wanna talk about, and people don't usually like that, especially if it's coming from a woman.'

'I had a person message me and engage in a conversation, telling me how and who I should be and what I should do as DJ Fuckoff, and they were telling me to stop sexualising myself,' Zoe recalls. 'They were just saying how I could be better than using sex to sell my music. I don't get why he felt he had this kind of authority. I wouldn't message anyone telling them how to be or what to do. I think it came from a sense of maybe thinking they were helping me, but DJ Fuckoff is my expression.' I asked her if she thinks this same guy would go and send a message to a man who writes equivalent sexual lyrics. 'No way,' she spits. 'It just wouldn't happen. I don't think that's ever happened. I don't imagine any man has ever said to another man to stop talking about all this sexual stuff. It's just crazy how it's just a whole different idea when women do it, and why they do it. People follow me because they like my music; maybe some people like the sexy posts too but this is all part of it. This is what makes me feel good. I want people to feel empowered and feel good, especially women. I want them to feel fuckin' hot, sexy, like they can do it too. This is how I go through all my emotions and failings, and if it's sexual, it is the way it is.'

She told me how she transformed this online situation into material, writing the track 'Death By Pussy': 'Death to all these people by pussy.' Zoe says that she feels supported by the people who attend nights, fellow DJs and promoters, and people who wish to dance and make music in a safe environment, but online, this can become a different situation. 'I did a product review of some new CDJs and in the comments section, a lot of guys were saying I had a stupid name; they were saying things like "Good luck getting booked but nice review." It's so pointless but with the name DJ Fuckoff it gives you everything you need to know. It gives me the power to be comfortable and not care about this kind of stuff, and it also gives me the power to know I don't have to respond because everything is right in front of you. It's like, "You've been warned! I told you!"' I ask Zoe if there's an element of fun that comes out of courting potential controversy. 'It's always fun when people get pissed off at my music; I am pushing buttons. Art has a role in being provocative, and yes, I feel what I'm doing is provocative. I like to make people get out of their comfort zone and I think it's important to be pushing this instead of how society is telling women how to act, what they should wear. I want to fucking break this, I want to push this, I want to test this. And if this is challenging for some people, maybe they're getting pushed, but then also maybe they think, actually, maybe this isn't so bad, maybe she can express herself like this, just as men do if they want.'

Zoe's online experiences at the receiving end of misogyny are far from unique for female, non-binary and trans DJs and producers. As a very broadly speaking cis identifying man, I am often blind to the weight that women undergo dealing with toxic masculinity. In the electronic music world, despite value placed on the dancefloor as a safe space, toxic masculinity manifests particularly (but not only) online, and one of the most common forms is in the casting of suspicion over the abilities of female and female-identifying artists. The 'Death By Pussy' origin story Zoe recollects reminds me of something another DJ/producer from Berlin, who in this case wished to remain anonymous, told me. This happened after posting selfies on her Instagram. 'A man online was messaging me saying, "If you don't want people to think you have a ghost producer, then you should post more pictures from your studio." Roman Flügel never posts anything out of his studio, but people would never assume he has a ghost producer. It›s ridiculous.' The unwillingness of this man to accept her autonomy that somehow her posting selfies called into question her ability as a producer feeds into the narrative that reinforces male-dominated line-ups and opportunities. Zoe herself has mentored for Femme Bass Mafia, a local initiative aiming to provide a safer space for women, trans and non-binary people for the learning and prac-tising of DJing. Another collective, No Shade, broadly based in Neukölln, runs training programs and party nights.

However, in a strange moment of irony, the first time we got onto this subject, back that afternoon in the summer, two guys along from us on the bench told us we were being too loud and asked if we could lower our voices. 'I don't think I'm good at talking quiet,' Zoe told me. I told her that I don't think I am either. These few months later, as we wind up our conversation in Prenzlauer Berg, she drops the bomb that she's been booked to play Panorama Bar. I think of a mix she posted on SoundCloud called 'Warning' and I get a premonition of hearing something like it as the sun rises across those windows upstairs inside. I think of tribalistic UK bass, aggressively pro-pulsive breakbeats, sirens and synth oscillations. Subtly inter-woven half-speed dub frequencies, acid pulses. I hear recall on my own memories back in the south of England. The early nineties. Following the directions along A roads. Sound systems in old barns and dilapidated farmhouses. The smell of generators heating up against damp grass.

I ask Zoe if there is a particular track that takes her back to being a child that reminds her of dancing with her mum and dad in the psy-trance parties of Auckland. And maybe of her dad's record store along the K Road. 'Yes! Yeah yeah yeah!' she says within a heartbeat, reaching out her phone, nails scanning instinctively along the cracked screen like they've done this a million times before. The smell of petrol is gone, Prenzlauer is calm again and our coffees are drunk. Her phone speaker facing upwards. She presses play.

4.

IN STILLNESS

KMRU. AMBIENCE. NAIROBI. MOABIT. PSYCHO & PLASTIC. FIELD RECORDING.

A bunker of a studio in London. Luke Slater, veteran electronic music producer, is sitting at a desk. Cabinets of modular synthesisers are attached to the wall around him, mysterious sound-generating boxes without monitors, without keyboards. Instead of the flicker of yellow pulses of light, we could be on a submarine. He makes adjustments across the machinery and, somewhere within the dials and switches routed together across a switchboard of primary coloured cables, the sound of a drone is generated.

There's never really a beginning or an end to a drone. There's just where you get on, and a thousand kilometres east, the drone arrives into the empty industrial space of Halle am Berghain. The drone circulates through cracked floor tiles and under silos that could have been built to funnel grain and could be easily mistaken, when looking up, for part of the club's immaculate sound system. Eighteen metres below, two figures are stood behind a desk. They receive the drone, which, as they do, is now growing in dimension and texture as it travels through their connected equipment.

On the left, KMRU, an alchemiser when it comes to processing ambience into emotional resonance, FFP2 mask and a box-fresh raincoat, guides the drone through his mixer, along the way adding texture, accentuations, ambience. I hear an echo of what could be a stone hitting a railway track. Or the clattering of dishes in a full sink. Next to him, Speedy J, ditto untarnished apparel and FFP2, who since the early nineties has helped carry Detroit influences into Europe, is adding what he calls accents, sudden events.

Ghostly shards of light from the factory windows shimmer across their cloaked forms like a visual reverb that accompanies the drone, field recorded grains, echoed oscillations and delayed pops as they fill up the space. As time progresses, exactly who is nurturing which sound becomes less and less clear, but the process of listening, reacting, adding, subtracting is the same as if they were a jazz trio. Collectively, they're improvising.

Later, as I talk with KMRU, one the city's more recent residents, he will use the word jamming. Jamming – how divisive is this word? But still, Jamming. Improvising. What's the difference? The three are in the flow of a beat-less musical exchange. The project was initiated during lockdown by Slater, with the recorded dialogue as 'a series of musical letters passed back and forth.' If world events had played differently, this collaboration might have taken place with the three producers playing in the same space amidst a live audience of more people than a small production crew. Then again, without the heightened need to reach out and communicate in whatever way possible, this collaboration maybe wouldn't have even been dreamt up. As it is, there is a certain circularity to not just the music but to the location. The album *Dialogue* had already been released on A-TON, the subsidiary for ambient and archive music run by Ostgut, being both the label owned by Berghain as well as the name of the club held in a disused railway repair depot that would close in 2003 before reopening, not far from here, the next year, as Berghain. But for now, on this day in August 2021, the dancefloor in the main room next door, and upstairs from that, its slightly lighter, slightly more housey sister, Panorama Bar, remains closed. This is the era when that giant banner by Thai artist Rirkrit Tiravanija hung down across the exterior of this former heating plant in simple black and white, reading *Morgen Ist Die Frage* – Tomorrow Is The Question. Unlike the banners of protest that have always hung across the squats and politicised WGs across the stadt that are clear in intention and succinct – the banners that stand for a Free Palestine and to Destroy Capitalism, *Morgen Ist Die Frage* to me felt like a gasp of uncertainty, a giant 'Fuck!!' It was as if a giant cartoon speech bubble was coming out of the mouth of a building whose pulse had never, over any weekend, not since people started arriving there to dance in 2004, stopped. Silence.

'In Berlin, I became more aware of the sense of silence,' Joseph Kamaru, the artist who is KMRU, tells me. It's a cold winter afternoon. We're having a conversation inside a Viennese-style restaurant that doubles as a bookshop in Moabit, near where he's lived for about a year now. 'I moved to Berlin during winter. It was lockdown and where I'm from in Nairobi, the noise level is higher than here. And here . . .' – he gestures to outside the restaurant window, where muted traffic crawls by – 'these cars passing and not being able to hear them is something that I wouldn't experience.'

Joseph is wearing a warm, orange-coloured beanie and as I arrive, he's finishing up a meeting over a project that may happen next year. With everyone I've met lately, there is that air of uncertainty of how future projects may or may not happen, but also a growing casualness to this, restrictions or no restrictions, online or with an audience. People find a way. His colleague leaves, doffs a hat and says with a twinkle, 'Stay Negative.' Joseph asks how I am and I tell him that I'm fine but that I got busted by a guard on the S-Train for not buying a ticket. He offers a gentle laugh. Joseph talks gently, smiles gently, has a thoughtful way of considering, sometimes reconsidering how to elaborate on a topic the more we discuss. This could be the academic in him. In Nairobi, before the pandemic, he taught at a university; right now, he's studying for a masters in Berlin. This could also be down to how listening has become part of his life and art. Listening is at the root of KMRU's music. Sometimes, as a field recordist, he will head out across the city to find textures and hidden resonances. The metallic sound the disused rail tracks that run through Park am Gleisdreieck make when they're tapped percussively. The shifting dynamics of a walkway along the canal. Often, he will initially explore areas without a recording device, giving time for his ears to understand the sounds, their history, the responsibility of borrowing from an environment. 'There's so much in our environment that we're missing out on,' he says. 'And for me, I try to implement this in my music in a way that I can be able to get the sounds heard.' At home, he pins up locations where something has sparked curiosity on a map to return to at a later date, this time with a Zoom H6 digital recorder.

We talk about the keynote sounds to a city, the contrasts between Berlin and Nairobi. 'And also for me,' he tells me, 'it's strange that I can't hear bird sounds in the morning compared to home.' Perhaps the most obvious of these keynotes to come to mind are the U-Bahn and S-Bahn. I think of records where the carriage's electrical drones have been sampled: Paul Kalkbrenner's 'Train', from the film *Berlin Calling*, which transforms the three-note bleep that lets you know the door is closing into an optimistic sunrise-arms-aloft hook-line. Or how about Oliver Koletzki's 'U-Bahn', which scatters subtle train samples underneath sophisto-melancholic synth-pop, the lyrics a humorous faux grumpy Berliner take on tunnels smelling like cigarette butts, dirt and tar, and how by sharing the same space inside, from bankers to junkies, we all become the same. Sonically, the U- and S-Bahn are as ubiquitous to Berlin as the *matatu* is to Nairobi.

'I grew up in the Kariokor Flats housing development, a neighbourhood which was very close to the city centre, and the main way to get about was to pay a very few coins and take the *matatu*,' Joseph says. The sounds on board *matatus* – privately owned, customised busses – amped into the foreground of Joseph's environment as he was growing up. The main and most affordable way to get around the city, each bus is an individually decorated, spray-painted street art shrine of loud pop culture juxtapositions. Inside, buses are often decked out with a sound system, free Wi-Fi, some show movies. The drivers act as music curators: in the morning, there might be gospel, easing passengers into the day ahead, switching to strands of East African techno styles for the flow of youth across midday onwards. More than mere transport, *matatus* are for when you don't have money to go to a club. 'The matatus gave a sense of being in a very lively connection with the social things that are happening, so much that you can't pay attention to one specific thing.'

There are field recordings on Joseph's computer of both Nairobi and Berlin transport. He mentions an idea he chews around, playing them both together and creating new spaces between them. 'Things were just happening so fast around me, you wouldn't be able to think of what you really want to do. You're just like, "Yeah, it's day", and you go and make things happen,' he reflects. 'In school, there was a lot of noise and then when I was sixteen or eighteen, my family decided to move to a different neighbourhood, further away from the city.' Outside of the bustle of inner-city living, in the district of Rongai, he says: 'The dynamic changed and all of us weren't sure if we were going to cope with this new environment; it's beautiful and nice and super calm and it took some time for all of us just to cope with the presence of nature, living in a serene environment where things are slowed down.' He describes the silence itself as becoming deafening. 'I became more aware of stuff I had around me; this is even before having a recorder.'

It was about this time the teenage Joseph started to understand more about his grandfather, Joseph Kamaru, the senior. In pre-school, teachers would play his grandfather's music, though he says, 'I understood listening to my grandfather's music as more of a fun thing, I didn't think it was very serious. Even the fact that we were learning his music in school, for me, it was just like, "Yeah, it's my grandfather."'

'I started becoming more and more aware in high school, where my teachers knew there was a Kamaru in the school and they wanted to figure out if I'm related to *the* Joseph Kamaru.' Activist musician. Person of the people. At the peak of his powers, the music of his grandfather, Joseph Kamaru, directly affected social change. In the fifties, he was as a street hawker, a house-help and a fruit seller, saving money to afford his first guitar. By the seventies and eighties, he became personal friends with Kenyan presidents, and then at other times, when things needed to be spoken out, he sang critically about the government. One song, 'Ndari ya Mwarimu', highlighted widespread sexual harassment of students in the educational system. The song outraged the teachers' union so much that they threatened a national strike, forcing parliament into a debate. 'I didn't relate deeper into his music until I was at university,' Joseph says. 'We had classes where we were learning about the colonial time and the music. And what his music did is mentioned in most texts. From conversations with my professors, I realised, okay, he's not only my grandfather but he's an important figure for the whole community in Kenya.'

'So it prompted me to meet him more and have conversations, which brought us very close together. I shared his name and he figured that I'm his grandson interested in music too. He used to come to my mom's place and just talk to me, or we'd jam together on the guitar.' Joseph Kamaru, the senior, passed in 2018. Now, Joseph has an archive project, releasing his grandfather's music across Bandcamp. 'We always wanted to work on some music together and after he passed, I felt a need to do something that would keep on sharing his music to the world, a way that his music could still stay alive.'

About a year before, I sat down with Joseph that cold November afternoon in an old-fashioned Moabit restaurant. As Joseph was just arriving in Berlin and beginning the next several years of his studying for a masters in Sound Art, adjusting his ears to the differences between Nairobi and Berlin, I was becoming attached to his music, specifically through *Peel*, an album of his made earlier that year during the first stretch of pandemic life. 'I lost my job. I was teaching guitar but with the pandemic there were fewer lessons, and I was also teaching sound in our university, and that ended. I was now crossing fingers on how my musical life is going to be,' Joseph tells me, as steam from a pot of green tea whisps upwards. '*Peel* came out of being confined since March of that year, all the way till August, just being around home and not moving much.'

As with the live performance at Halle am Berghain, *Peel* begins with two drones emerging out of silence. There is a soft cylindrical quality to the textures as they gradually expand and echo, like an unhurried bell ringing from a distant window. *Peel*, a record he never planned to make, recorded on one day and in one live take during lockdown, was a continuation of practices Joseph had been exploring for some time. Yet, it arrived into a beat-less world and was received with a response that more than surprised him. There was the end of year polls, the sudden international recognition. But on a more interpersonal level, it felt rooted in an emotional resonance of something we were all experiencing. 'I got so many people writing to me how *Peel* has taken them through very weird and difficult times,' he says, 'and I just don't know how to feel about it because it's so overwhelming, in a good way.' He confesses to trying to understand what happened with a record he hadn't even planned to make. 'I was playing that record again and again and trying to see how it reached so many people. It's a whole thing that I just didn't expect.'

Weird and difficult times. Personally, *Peel* reached me during that elongated winter lockdown where, for seven months, the city, such a flowing organism of movement, stood still. Shops closed. Benches locked and upturned. Cafes one in, one out. The vaccines existed, yet for the most part, supply hadn't reached Berlin. I was living in my tenth apartment since moving here, a cosy old box up on the fourth floor of a creaky *Altbau* in Bergmannkiez, the slower, more genteel, almost Schönebergian side of Kreuzberg. Over winter, the heating would click, the refrigerator would hum. I found these sounds comforting; they became like pets.

I'd hear Erik Satie from out of the window. Someone was learning 'Gnossienne No. 1' on piano and each week, whoever was learning would get a little better, occasionally having an off day, hitting bum notes; maybe their attention would be lost elsewhere. I felt rooted in their progress, like a spectator at the side of a park football match. The building had noise issues; uninsulated walls are common for older buildings and most of the tenants were jammed in various states of lockdown. We all lived in the overlap of each other's sonic

domain. I'd frequently get woken by the sounds of a chef getting home from his night shift directly above my head. His
late-night sessions sounded like furniture being dragged across
floorboards; wine bottles would drop and then roll across my
ceiling. Dealers would buzz and then quickly exit through the
night. He kept cocaine hours. Still, there was good: Trump
had just been voted out, I'd hear Satie out the window, and
during this time, I started listening to *Peel*, and consequently
whatever else I could stream by KMRU. It was as if his work's
contemplative, beat-less nature took on a wider space across a
world without its usual sonic geography. No dancing in clubs,
no tables of people in cafes and bars conversing, no clinking
of glasses. Instead, KMRU's SoundCloud Bluetoothed across
that little box of mine up in Bergmannkiez.

I think of the cocaine chef and how Joseph mentioned, back
in those teenage years, once he and his family had moved out
of the inner city to the comparatively serene Rongai, sounds
that were bad became worse and that all sounds – good, bad,
indifferent – took on more dimension. 'Sonically, I could dis-
tinguish and separate different sounds in the environment as
the sounds became so precise,' he said. Before, when Joseph
was living near the city centre, the textures he'd experienced
daily would layer up. In the confined space of a *matatu* bus,
sound could, in theory, be emanating from as many sources
as there are people. Then add to this the onboard sound system, the possibility, too, of audio from movies playing on the
attached widescreen TVs. I think of a multichannel digital
audio workstation, as if each channel has sound recorded onto
it and each channel is playing simultaneously. With everything

playing at once, individual qualities get lost or at least lose their full resonance. A wall of noise. But then take a fresh folder with mostly blank channels and what sounds are there become more pronounced. 'There's a precision of things in their place. Maybe it's because of the slowness,' Joseph says. 'Going back to when I started, when I bought the first recorder and putting my headphones on, it's an exciting feeling to hear more and control how much you can hear. It's like having binoculars and seeing further.'

'You're using the microphone as new pairs of your ears, but unlike ears, you can control them,' Joseph explains. 'I used to sing in high school, and when I finished, that's when I just discovered that you can make music on laptops. I was using my dad's computer and slowly, given the environment changed how I was listening to music or the direction in which I wanted to make music, I bought my Zoom digital recorder. Then being out, listening and realising how loud our environment is, I thought, "Wow." So for me, the recorder was this device that triggered a sense of there being more songs out there. I was recording so much, just being present with everything that can make a sound and then trying to make a narrative, maybe this desk . . .' he taps the table. It sounds thinner than oak but chunkier than plastic. I hear an elderly group sitting near us, their voices rosy from afternoon wine. Nearby a waiter drops a spoon.

We talk about being present. Joseph acknowledges that there are meditative qualities to his music. Textures that could be considered ambient. During various stages of the pandemic, the works of other artists exploring beat-less, contemplative sounds felt heightened. One night, I went to the Kraftwerk factory and caught the Manchester/Berlin-based artists Space Afrika performing at the remodelled Berlin Atonal festival. There was an energy in the audience during their set that felt heightened. As if over the course of the pandemic, something had shifted. Re-wired. Even with MCs onstage and occasional snatches of drum and bass rhythm, Space Afrika's set was largely beat-less, textures floated, grains went deep. Yet the energy in the crowd was propulsive, wired. In our label-based world, Space Afrika, like KMRU, can get described as ambient but the emotion that left the stage that night and the way we all absorbed it felt expressive of something definitions of ambient don't take account of. I heard sadness, anger, the urgency of pirate radio and a Mancunian off-kilter lyricism you hear in Shaun Ryder, in Factory Records, in the poet John Cooper Clarke.

I started to wonder if the way ambient music is felt had undergone a shift. When Brian Eno took captainship of the term in 1978, his sleeve notes for 1978's *Ambient 1: Music For Airports* described the music as something 'designed to induce calm and space to think'. A kind of aural furniture. Eno suggested a deliberate lack of attachment to the music that it could serve as functional background. Or if it did have an emotional function, it was to soothe. This is how ambient had been living these past forty years. Ambient before the pandemic had reached middle-age and was equally comfortable living in a New Age, patchouli-scented dimension as it had been in the sleekness boutique design of a kind of luxury living, like hotels and wellness retreats. Soft focus and in the background. A typical cis babyboomer, ambient was never given encouragement to explore its own complex web of emotions or examine where it came from. This middle-aged ambientness had been something I enjoyed floating in from time to time.

I think of a moment visiting Liquidrom, a wellness spa several kilometres east along the Spree from where Joseph and I sat and spoke that winter afternoon. I am with a group of people and we have just left the scalding heat of an *Aufguss* ceremony, where a *Saunermeister* has whipped a towel that circulates intense scented heat around our nude bodies. I leave, crossing a snowy courtyard, in heightened sensation from the contrast of heat to cold. Then, across the other side on Liquidrom, I float in a salted pool, its low domed roof darkened except for a muted skylight, calm except for the sounds the water makes from people floating in semi-darkness. Somewhere nearby me, I hear a couple press into each other and groan. But most of the people around are just floating. I stretch my arms out into near-darkness, dip my ears back below the surface and I hear soft electronic music. The music is coming from underwater speakers and the sounds are ambient in the most traditional sense, selected to float in. And I float in it. I am utterly happy to ignore the ersatz qualities of its nineties slowed down hip hop beats and synth pads and just be present, happy but free of emotional baggage, and float in this forty-plus-year-old form of ambience curated to match these surroundings.

But then, the world silenced. Thomas Tichai, tall, genial, bright orange jacket and retro check shirt, is framed in Zoom from his studio/living space in that most northern district of Pankow. He is one half of electronic project Psycho & Plastic, whose sound changed to reflect the emotional and the physical realities of lockdown. 'In February 2020,' he tells me, 'we'd been set up to play club shows and we were gearing up for new productions and it was all kind of club-focused.'

His creative partner, Alexandre Decoupigny, has just joined us on Zoom now from a separate screen. They had both followed a trajectory that began a decade earlier after Thomas and Alexandre relocated to Berlin from studying music in Liverpool, where they both picked up an extremely rare quality in two German gentlemen of being able to spontaneously turn on excellent Scouse accents. The pair made contact with me in 2014 when I was writing a blog, and they, possibly caught by the Can-referencing name I'd given it – Tago Mago – dropped me some of their music, which had a tinge of the krautrock about it. Over the years, we've developed a friendship and I've watched their music, whilst still in many ways on the outside of any kind of big momentum, grow a cult following.

'And then in March,' Alexandre, also genial and also very tall, says, 'as you all know, everything stopped and all the clubs closed and all the venues and the audiences that we were making music with suddenly, well, in a way, they disappeared.' Not only that but so too did his desire to make kinetic music. Into that first lockdown, he tells me, 'We had a lot of new, unknown and unresolved things going through our heads and feelings going through our hearts.'

The last time I saw both Thomas and Alexandre together in the flesh was around this time. Thomas had prepared a spread in his flat and we were all lamenting the recent passing of Andrew Weatherall. The duo had recently been played on Weatherall's

NTS Radio show, and like his sets, their cosmic-disco infused electronica had a chug about it. I didn't know, though, that this, annually, was an emotionally delicate time for Alexandre. 'Around that time every year my body remembers the trauma of my mom dying slowly and then finally the dying in 2014,' he says, recalling a time just before lockdown, when the pair got together again; they cooked food, played video games, hung, and for once didn't make music, but were there for each other, Thomas supporting Alexandre. 'And Thomas asked me, so what does that sound like? The way you feel in your body? I just thought, wow, everything feels quiet around us in the pandemic. And I could listen to myself. And so I sat down and started playing and tried to give him a musical answer to the question.'

In silence, do we hear our emotions louder? There was never any grand plan to make an ambient record. Still, the music on the duo's album *Placid House* came together through social distancing, passing tracks in progress backwards and forwards between their separate set-ups in Pankow and Schöneberg. They left thumping rhythms back in a world that had stopped, and they used ambience to tap into emotion. Less drone-based and more melodically arranged than KMRU's *Peel*, their own personal response to the situation reminds me, in its gaping beat-less synth melancholia, of Tangerine Dream. I think back to Mark Reeder describing when he moved to Schöneberg in the late seventies and would listen to their album, *Rubycon*: the atmospheric music seeming to exist in the desolate streets and hippy fug of the Schöneberg that Tangerine Dream came from. I remember the stillness, too, of that first lockdown when both *Placid House* and *Peel* were birthed.

5.

COCKAIGNE

ZIÚR. FRIEDRICHSHAIN. ATONAL. UTOPIAS.

'Some of you are still sitting down,' Ziúr says, appearing from out of the darkness behind a small stage, tiny in comparison to the vastness of our surroundings. She has a mic in one hand, the other spinning CDJs, their pin-sharp LEDs light up her long, tie-dyed T-shirt and longer hair into ectoplasmic green. For the last hour, we've been floating horizontally.

'Well, that won't fly,' she says. A frequency jolts us into movement. Out of speakers stacked column-high, the frequency has the belly-thump of dub. It has fragmented kick drums and disembodied harmonies that swarm across us like ghosts out of the Ark of the Covenant. The artist onstage is playing the title track from an album that pays homage to a mythical utopia, captured sporadically in books, songs and pictures since the Middle Ages.

The album, *Antifate*, made over two months during the pandemic, is only a small portion of a prolific output she's released into the world during the same year. *Antifate* summons up the mythical land of Cockaigne: a utopia where peasants can be free, where wine flows and houses are made of cake. Yet over a time when the pandemic has kept clubs closed and the options to share communal dancing with others has been restricted, a moment like this, where for the first time in eighteen months I am maskless moving inside with more people than I can estimate, feels like I've arrived in this mythical land.

But I am not; I am in a deactivated power plant. A repurposed furnace. It's a Sunday night late into September and Ziúr is onstage for the opening of Metabolic Rift, a corona-age reimagining of the long-running Berlin Atonal festival. The festival started in 1982 as a way of gathering disparate noisemakers and musical anarchists; dubbed by the press that noticed them as the 'Berlin disease', Atonal was the baby of young Westphalian Dimitri Hegermann. Amongst other things, Hegermann played bass in a project called Leningrad Sandwich, and was intrigued by a day festival that had taken place the previous year: Festival Genialer Dilettanten.

Unlike this previous year's anarchic bash, where fuzzy VHS video exists and is on YouTube, there is very little documented evidence of what happened at the first Atonal. There are the names of people, groups, collectives that played: Psychic TV, Z'EV, Test Dept, Club Moral, The Anti Group, Laibach, Minus Delta T, Clock DVA. Then there is the apocryphal tale of Einstürzende Neubauten's jackhammer going berzerk backstage. And the location: the still-standing SO36 in Kotti.

A few years ago, the festival moved to this deactivated power plant. Approaching the Kraftwerk factory tonight, on my way along Köpenicker Straße, I look upwards an ocean liner-height above. Two huge chimneys, now ornamental, once coughed out hot mechanical excretions across the Spree, back when this factory powered heating for East Berlin. The mechanisms inside, long since deactivated, were activated sixty years before, over a period of time where East Germany was building and rebuilding, honing in the Wall amid a forty-year monumental ghosting to the West.

As I show my vaccine pass to the friendly guy that scans it, I wonder if this is where the workers at the Mitte CHP Plant would queue up, if they indeed queued up to begin shifts. The last time I was here, lost in something like unrequited love with a friend, we queued to get inside Tresor. We were Friday night drunk, skint and ready to spend our last euros to dance. I was lost in the belief that our out-of-sync feelings would somehow align. This never happened. Our energy got weird, too weird to be standing in a queue of hyped-up partygoers. Then a few weeks later, the gates locked, and you know the rest.

But here we are; it's a Sunday night late into September. Today there's an election and Angela Merkel is stepping down. New regulations have allowed club spaces to reopen without restriction for the vaccinated, and for the first time in eighteen months, this vast old power station reopens. I go through up a staircase where yellow beams cast us into expressionistic shadows and up into the vastness of Turbine Hall, and for some time before Ziúr appears, I bathe in ambience.

Now onstage, Ziúr moves in front of her desk and sings the words 'This is the air you breathe.' Beats fly across the hall in fragments, chopped and screwed, ghosts of R&B, ghosts of what could even have been once eighties pop samples buried deep within machinery. Yes, 'this is the air you breathe,' she sings, and I am breathing. We are all breathing each other's air again. I reconnect with those incidental minutiae: the spontaneous energy currents between people in toilet queues. How couples stand by each other when they listen to a live performance. How difficult it is to squeeze through people without spilling a plastic cup. The sheer weirdness of normality. Onstage, Ziúr is no longer alone. Tiny, furious, Kianí Del Valle, choreographer and collaborator dressed in shiny green plastic, her platted hair jolting far and wide through machinic yet graceful spasms, her moves dueting with Ziúr's splintered beats.

The two are panting, exhilarated. Cockaigne tonight is manifesting as a kiss-ass punk rock group. Ziúr reaches for Kianí's hand, they both grip onto each other. Both are pushing each other forward, both pushing each other through. I sense graft. I sense love. I sense a shared journey. Both are travellers and Berlin is a destination, but it is not their Cockaigne.

Kianí grew up with salsa, reggaeton. She remembers those first warm experiences of music and movement through her parents in Puerto Rico. Her dad playing along to the vinyl at home with his congas, her mum dancing, shaking her ass and screaming. In Montreal, she studied choreography, dancing ballet and contemporary. Working as a door girl, she got introduced to electronic music. She's choreographed videos and performances for Lotic, Floating Points and Dirty Projectors. Her own collective, the KDV Dance Ensemble, has reimagined contemporary dance as a rootless, migratory experience soundtracked by her electronic collaborators. Kianí, Like Ziúr, is never not working. Ziúr, unlike Kianí, does not talk about the specifics of where she is from.

When I finally moved to Berlin in 2018, Ziúr lived a few *Altbau* apart along the same straße in Friedrichshain as I did. This was a little while after the release of her debut LP, *U Feel Anything?*, released on the long-established leftfield electronic label, Planet Mu. Although we didn't initially know each other, we shared the constant sound of drilling from never-ending roadworks, the hot smell of tarmac and the same *Späti*.

'I just don't want to talk about nationalities and stuff like that, but I grew up in a small town,' she had told me the first time we met. This was during a blizzard, inside the warmth of an old-fashioned cafe on Karl-Marx-Allee. 'If I can just make some ground rules in general,' she had said. 'My regular name is of no interest. I don't want to talk about my background and no nationalities. I think these are just things that put me in boxes and I don't want to go there.'

We sat on white chairs, snow outside, wine bottles displayed across white shelves, the sound of a baby crying weaving in and out of my recording of the interview as I listen back. I was fresh to the city, interviewing her for my podcast and perhaps a little uncalibrated in my sensitivity. On reflection, I was fishing towards an area of her life that she had previously kept publicly quiet. 'I just don't like boxes in general. I don't like to be categorised within certain frameworks that people consider being important for themselves or for something. I don't like these sorts of things. Then there's the whole no nations, no borders approach of what I think the world should be working as. I have big problems with national pride. For me, it's more interesting to keep it open.'

What she did share, though, is that she'd grown up in a secluded straight white environment. 'It's really important that I will never go back. I don't ever want to go back to the point where I'm this limited to how the world turns out to be,' she said. 'And obviously it matters, your upbringing matters and where you grew up matters to a certain extent. It's not like one hundred per cent we'll not talk about it if we're having a private conversation. Still, I may phrase it in a certain way. Sometimes my answers vary from saying I'm an Earth citizen, but that's become a little bit too hippie for me right now. I'd say I'm from the internet but the internet is getting on my nerves too.'

We talked about the need to break away from orthodoxy. Orthodox approaches to life and orthodox approaches to creativity. Years before manifesting the digital resonances of her identity as Ziúr, as a young punk in an unnamed town, stifling effects permeated through those early jams and rehearsal room sweatboxes. 'I was working with people that were really good at shredding the perfect guitar solo. The thing is, they don't necessarily have the good ideas, and I had to realise this when it comes to being creative.' She pauses. 'I do think I have a bunch of talent, but I'm not necessarily the school type of person. For example, I don't know what a note is.'

Once we spoke from her studio set-up, arranged into an L-shape in the corner of her flat. She was swivelled round to face me, behind her a giant monitor. There were decks, boxes of hardware, a midi keyboard wired up, and in between the cables that run around an ashtray are the tokens of a time before she made electronic music as Ziúr: a bass guitar, the cut and paste art of a punk record sleeve. As Ziúr, she works without a formula, connecting with intuition. 'It's more of a . . . not really a jam but I'm dealing with a lot of chance, whatever sound comes next. I'm just like, maybe I'll use this, maybe play around with it, maybe change it later but I still try to maintain a flow, and then it's very intuitive.'

'Early on, I was always singing because that's what I could do on my own. I did this for a while and then at some point, it was also happening later in Berlin that I tried for lots of years to work with a friend on music projects. We tried all different types of things and it never worked out; it was always a weird vibe. And then one time we had a bunch of people gathered, in a band practice, and we were trying a new project and it was a really, really terrible project. At some point, I just couldn't take it anymore. I grabbed a guitar and realised that I had a whole different way of influencing what was going on. Just because I grabbed this instrument that I didn't know how to play, even though it was familiar because I had a guitar since forever. Even though I had a really funny way of playing, it was somehow resonating with people, and we practised in this space. There were some people who were also really good at shredding the perfect guitar solo, but they were looking at me, like, "I don't know how she can do this." I could see these people being impressed and I'd still cover my ears when they were playing guitar.'

I tell her that I didn't gravitate towards music at school because if you didn't learn the scales, or have parents that invested in buying you a violin or giving you piano lessons, you were unofficially excluded. I knew even at an early age that the pop music I loved came from a different approach, but there was no educational impetus to connect with whatever that was. Growing up in a small town, we had our shred dudes, too. Those shreds can be very impressive, but I always felt like they were competing. For Ziúr, having finally found an approach in which she could be guided by intuition, she'd meet with her friend in a practice space away from the other people. Here, 'My friend started playing drums and I started playing guitar for the first time, and then all of a sudden, we did a record and a European tour. Those other solo shred dudes are still in their little small town in the same shitty bar from twenty years ago being in a Foo Fighters covers band or something.'

I hear myself chortle like a pig, listening back to that moment. We started talking about spirituality, being careful to circumnavigate the woo-woo. Maybe it's because I hear something fluid, ritualistic, even pagan in her music. That first LP, *U Feel Anything?*, opens with 'Human Life Is Not A Commodity', a piece that felt to me as if it had been glazed in some form of hyper-digital mysticism. The pitched vocals of collaborator Aïsha Devi on 'Body Of Light' echo back to that mention of hers about coming from the internet: I think of the PC Music fluidity of A.G. Cook.

A few nights prior, a giant supermoon hung across Karl-Marx-Allee. Seeing it, I felt an eerie stillness across the straße. Karl-Marx-Allee has a feeling of being frozen in another time as it is, wide and designed to give splendour to a country and a belief system that no longer exists. 'I was in a car and I tried to take a picture of the moon,' she says, 'and it didn't work but it was fucking huge and so shiny.' Sometimes a moon doesn't like to be photographed, I joke. 'I think so; it's like me basically.' So are you camera shy? 'No,' she says, 'I'm just picky with the results.'

We've met a handful of times, sometimes formally: with my digital recorder placed in between us over a coffee table. Me asking questions for my podcast or a magazine. Her, engaging fully each time with a mixture of sweet sincerity and a frankness that seems incapable of glossing over the bull-shit, romanticise a picture. Sometimes, we'd run into each other in the *kiez*, maybe I'd just popped out to the *Späti* to buy a Sunday pack of Funny Frisch; we were neighbours after all. Every encounter, whether we've discussed groceries or the socio-politics of collectives, the same frankness burns out of her. She can say things that sound both funny and cynical, yet at the same time sweet and utterly full of love towards those around her and to anyone else that is able to be present and open. At the end of the set at Kraftwerk, dripping with sweat and having rocked a crowd, she gave love through her mic to Kianí, to Sander Houtkruijer, who created the visuals in a way so heartfelt. When I asked her if she'd be up for speaking with me again, for this, a book about Berlin, there was a moment of caution. After all, she far from romanticises this city. 'Berlin is a shit show too, you know,' she had said, a resident here for over fifteen years. 'It's just that other places are way less attractive.'

For Ziúr, moving to Berlin didn›t come down to any notion of this being ‹the place to be›. She came for love, a romantic relationship. And to leave behind her job as a night manager, looking after the bands, making them sandwiches, running money with tour managers. In this club, she›d seen initial co-operative values to nurture a community worn away to the degree all everyone wanted to do was to cash up and go home each night. Utterly rare for such a long period of time, she still lives in the same apartment. Over that first hot summer, she spent most of that time fixing the place up.

'Friedrichshain aged really well; it's still as uncool as it was before,' she tells me, 'but back then, there was definitely more dog shit on the sidewalk. It was closer to being a punk neighbourhood.' Into this Nokia-powered era, Berghain, walking distance away, was relatively new and Easyjet had only started running flights, making the city newly accessible as a budget destination. Yet, gentrification wasn't a threat, or at least overtly. A friend told me that in 2005 he paid two hundred euros a month for a two-bedroom flat in Mitte. Weep.

Where we're sat now is quiet. The quietness can be a surprise to people in other areas who can, to be frank, make an assumption that all of Friedrichshain is a constant skirmish. Yet here, we're a distance away from the weekend market bustle around Boxhagener Platz and the night crawls of Berlin starter-pack tourists hanging out of Washauer Strasse hostels. 'It's always been a worker's neighbourhood' she says, 'just real people. Maybe now there's more families, but it's not too posh, it's kind of real. It's boring; it's usually quiet.' Even during the period where we lived on the same stretch of road in 2018, it felt to me a distinctly un-international neighbour-hood. A place where Berliners who were born Berliners live and where the local *Apotheque* - Fraüline Beckers – even has its own crinkly 16mm advert that runs pre-main feature in the local kino.

When we were neighbours, I found this *kiez* too quiet. I was in my Berlin honeymoon period, living for the first time in a new country and, unlike Ziúr, I most certainly had a Berlin romance I wanted to consummate. I wanted to escape Brexit and disentangle myself from anyone who could possibly not want to be part of Europe. Berlin, for me, was my Cockaigne and I confessed to her that this *kiez* felt too quiet. 'First of all, you've got to get to know a city,' she replied sagely. 'I started really early when I came here to open a restaurant, so I did this for a few years. When I started it, I didn't know the city well enough to figure out that maybe the area I opened it in wasn't the right one.'

The restaurant's neighbourhood was in Prenzlauer Berg, by then not the chi-chi swan in the north, yet no longer the raw squat land of reunification either. 'There were struggles with not knowing the city well enough and not having seen the progression in the city. This was a time when Prenzlauer Berg was dying, and also, it was a vegan restaurant. It was a little bit too radical for the normies and too clean for the punks. It was just a little bit too early for its time, whereas now it would be popping.'

'In the end, we lost a lot of money. It was my responsi-bility, and it was seen as a collective in a way, but I was in charge. It's always a sign that if you go to a restaurant and every two weeks there are different staff, you can tell it's ran badly. If you go through a lot of shit years and you have the same people opening and closing the place, then those people are sticking together.'

The importance of community reoccurs through our conversations. As a teenager, she tried Antifa, VoKü, over the years getting involved with many groups and political structures, never sticking long. 'There's always that one person dominating the narrative,' she told me. 'That's why I moved away from the punk scene back then. When I moved here, my old school friend lived in a squat. I thought, "Oh cool, I'll find open minds in a radical space," but it's not like that, posing as a subculture but having the same rules as normal society. I would cook there three times a week. I even helped renovate a practice space in the basement. People wouldn't say hi to me in the staircase or include me in dinner conversations because I didn't appear punk enough for them. I kind of like the romantic vision of punks.'

Shredders un-democraticising music jams, punks falling back on societal norms, style gatekeepers and apparel judgements, gentrification rent hikes separating communities. It has to be one of life's biggest downers that communities are so often under some kind of threat, often internal. But what about those moments when everything galvanises together? It was through a community space in another squat, this time the now institutionalised Schokoladen, just off Rosenthaler Platz in Mitte, that in 2012, she transformed from guitar to electronics. 'A friend was doing a Christmas event and she asked me to DJ. Everybody was doing a little bit of something and I decided that I'm going to write some music and perform it,' she recalls. 'So in four days, I wrote five songs and performed them and there was my new project.'

Ziúr was born. We were introduced initially through a mutual friend, Antonio, who used to attend Boo Hoo, the night she helped set up and run with DJ Joey Hansom. Boo Hoo was no labels and experimental and rooted in the values of being open. Mixing up sounds and styles, once a friend of hers played nothing but gospel records, and like Ziúr›s own DJ sets, which might on any occasion catapult from pop acapella to bloody noise, footwork to rave, again, an instinctive path, the nights didn›t adhere to any notion of dancefloor expectation.

I asked Antonio what he remembers about going to Boo Hoo. 'Those parties invited the most interesting producers and at the same time invited you to accept not only musical freedom but also your own personal one.' Relatively speaking, Antonio Cardenas is a Berlin veteran. A lockdown walk along the canal with him always involves bumping into people. Everyone knows Antonio; he has a smile that could end a war and a genuine agenda-free desire to help people come together. But back then, he was exploring places where, as a young Queer music lover, a newcomer from Venezuela, he felt at home.

'It was liberating,' Antonio told me on one of these walks. 'A first nightlife safe place, which became a beautiful home for me.' He talks about finding this freedom within Boo Hoo, as well as the much beloved Creamcake, which combined open values with an exploratory musical ethos that stepped out of the 4/4. In these nights, he experienced the energy of cutting-edge producers like Arca, Lotic and Paula Temple given free rein to follow ideas and intuition. 'For me, Boo Hoo being forward-thinking came from a musical freedom that I hadn't experienced before. You could play whatever, mix it with whatever else, and it somehow made sense. The genre was not defined, neither musically or from the people who attended the parties.'

Antonio told me one afternoon as we walked along Paul-Linke-Ufer, autumnal leaves falling into muddy heaps: 'You were welcome as you were, as long as you were respectful and open to whatever was happening. It was a safe space without having to say it was, as it happens nowadays. You met everyone who wanted to do something different. It was exciting to be there and witness what was happening. You could definitely feel it was unique, and I felt extremely privileged to be somehow part of it, as a viewer.'

When I spoke with Ziúr about Boo Hoo a couple of years ago, the night was winding down, the parties becoming less regular. No Instagram account and the last Facebook page entry dates back to December 2017. She emphasised things were moving on. Although Boo Hoo often got described as a Queer party, Ziúr was careful about any form of labelling. 'I mean, some people were saying it's a Queer party but we never had any labels,' she told me. 'We mostly wanted a really, really mixed audience and mixed line-up. We wanted to have a bunch of people coming together with a feeling of being welcome in a space. It being really important that people can just be themselves and it's okay to be you whoever you are.

Not so many events deliver that to be honest, there's always a little bit of "Oh, look at your sneakers." We just wanted people to be able to let go when they come. That's why we never want to label it. Because once you label it, it would be always exclusive in that sense, and we want the maximum amount of inclusivity.'

'That's why I don't want to always talk about certain things. I like confusion. I like to confuse people in general and make them make their own decisions in terms of not being preoccupied with a certain agenda.' I ask her if in confusing people you can encourage people to approach something with an open mind? 'They have no choice; they gotta think for themselves.' And is it possible to have a healthy relationship with someone if you don't agree with them? 'Probably,' she shrugs. 'I mean, I do mostly agree with my friends, but it's really important for me to provide the feeling to my friends that no matter how strange and weird they are in their certain loopy spirals, they're just welcome to be themselves when they're my friend. This also gives me the opportunity to relax and be one hundred per cent real.'

Sometimes there are elements of her music that remind me of what used to be called IDM – Intelligent Dance Music. Maybe it's the fragmented beats, the abrasiveness and abstraction, and then those ethereal textures. Maybe it's also because those first two albums were released on Mike Paradinas' Planet Mu. This label initially established itself in the nineties as a home for music often associated as IDM, before progressing onto championing movements that live and circulate more around the entire body like juke.

Similarly to IDM, Ziúr's productions extend club conventions to the outer limits of the dancefloor. Yet here we need to part with that comparison.

The term Intelligent Dance Music originated from an early nineties mailing list dedicated to artists found on Warp Records' *Artificial Intelligence* compilation. Calling it Intelligent Dance Music supposedly suggesting that this is serious music, made for listening but not so much dancing. As if also suggesting that music made specifically to dance to is not intelligent. Sonia Fernández Pan, the writer and podcaster I had connected with to talk about identity on the dancefloor, summed it up when she told me: 'It's like when white intellectual people do music it's intelligent, but when it's to dance to, what is it? A stupid music for dancing?'

By keeping the music in the head, as IDM implies, you remove the dancefloor, you remove the body and you remove the community. You make it all about the solo genius of the composer and how their work needs to be listened to, like, really listened to. Ziúr's music was born through community, and even though the vast body of her work is solo, it exists in connections between open-minded souls. It exists, like at Kraftwerk, in the bodies dancing out of hibernation (the club space's hibernation, if not the hibernation of everyone dancing; I'm well aware I'm late in the pandemic in dancing again).

Back in the Kraftwerk factory. I'm being a loner tonight. I came on my own and wasn't even sure I'd go until I put my shoes on and headed one step at a time out the door and onto the S-Bahn. Onstage, Ziúr and Kianí have just reached that moment together where their hands are held. Perspiring.

Pushing each other forward. Linked in unity. Even though Berlin isn›t filled with the same romantic allure for her as for so many who come here, in many ways, she *is* the Berlin dream.

An outsider rejecting the orthodox, creating community around her. When we had spoken about what friendship means, she finished by talking about how in being open and accepting people as who they are, only then do you get to live these real experiences with each other. And that real experiences aren't always pretty. The sweat and perspiration onstage at Kraftwerk isn't a team-building high-five exercise or some self-congratulatory 'Aren't we awesome?' thing. Is this actually what Cockaigne is?

6.

QUESTION ALL BORDERS

DANIELLE DE PICCIOTTO. NEW YORK. CHARLOTTENBERG. KOTTI. THE LOVE PARADE. GENIALE DILLETANTEN. DER HIMMEL ÜBER BERLIN.

Before Berlin, for Danielle, there was New York. And despite the fear of violence and the excesses of greed, there was the smell of chestnuts roasting along Seventh Avenue at dawn and the sounds the DJs played at the weekend. She loved studying and took as many classes as she could. She loved the 1920s and devoured literature about Paris and the Weimar Berlin of Brecht. And before that day in 1987, when she arrived up the stairs and into a Kreuzberg loft, for Danielle, there was New York.

'New York had this really magical atmosphere at dawn; it was still empty and I'd walk along Seventh Avenue and just marvel at the city,' she tells me. We're sat in her studio over four thousand kilometres east and thirty-five years later. Back then, Danielle De Picciotto was a teenager from Tacoma with a scholarship to study fashion. 'Because I was coming in from

Queens, you never knew if the subway was going to break down or not. And if it did, it could break down for hours, but I didn't mind getting up that early because walking along Manhattan that early in the morning had this really magical atmosphere.'

She had a place at the Fashion Institute of Technology in Manhattan. She loved fashion, or to be clear, the making clothes aspect of fashion rather than the industry aspect of fashion. 'I was at college from eight. I took as many classes as I could. You could take all the mandatory classes, but then you could also take all these other ones too – jewellery, design, papermaking – but then you could also do sociology and politics. And then the teachers at night . . .' – she pours green tea from an ornate china pot – 'The teachers at night were really good because they were people that worked during the day. So the person that was teaching sociology at night, he was working in a prison during the day. I usually took classes until around ten in the evening. Then, it wouldn't make sense to go all the way back to Queens.' Instead, Danielle would meet up with friends who had apartments in Manhattan. 'And then,' she says, 'we would go out either for a drink if it was during the week, or at the weekends we would just dance.'

'I went to a lot of clubs, but I was more into the garage scene and hip hop. I wasn't really into the underground music scene all that much before I got to Berlin,' she tells me. We're sat on pink armchairs arranged like a salon in the centre of her studio; the tea has just reached drinking temperature. There's a European lilt to the way she phrases certain words because Danielle is American, European and a nomad. There have been times she and her partner Alexander have fallen out of love with Berlin. Years travelling and living in different cities, hoping to capture what they felt Berlin was losing. And that moment on the Ku'Damm, dancing one rainy summer afternoon in '89. That moment, like a switch turning everything from monochrome to technicolour, is only part of it. Magic existed before this, and magic drew her in. And even before then, there was garage, there was hip hop and there was disco on the extravagant dancefloors of New York.

New Yorkers describe the mid-to-late eighties as both terrifying and optimistic. Both extremely dangerous and a mecca for a new kind of wealth. I asked Danielle about the clubs that she'd visit and, without hesitation, she mentioned two. 'Danceteria was my home-based club. I got to know the bouncer really well; he was living together with another friend of mine, so we'd spend a lot of time there.' An edgy three-floor hub of new wave and post-new wave nightlife open across the night from eight till eight.

'This was slightly before garage-house came out, Madonna had just become famous, but she was only just famous.' In fact, Danceteria is where Madonna made her first public appearance. The club had moved out of its original location (an illegal mafia liquor den) and became a place where you might catch The Birthday Party playing live if they were in town. Or you might see Basquiat, RuPaul, Lauper or Haring propping up the bar.

Contrastingly, a little south of her studies, Area was all fantasy. Yes, the main dancefloor DJs ignored forward trends and favoured playing long-established disco. However, what could have been just an eighties spin on Studio54 (which incidentally, by this point, had pretty much become a corporate sushi bar), was the sheer extravagance of the world inside.

'And this is what I really liked about Area back then,' Danielle reflects. 'It was a huge club and they would do huge decorations for it every couple of months. There were living models and they would turn the whole thing into a pool or into a jewel-encrusted palace or something completely out of this world.' Sometimes the owners would spend up to $60,000 transforming Area and they picked themes like Faith, centrepiece: a burning cross suspended over a swimming pool. They did a sci-fi lunar landscape and a Fellini party, and this one featuring banqueters eating seafood off a nude Magdalen Pierrakos. 'They spent a lot of money on it,' she says. 'It was the hottest club, and to get in was really, really difficult, but just the effort they made of transforming the place into some kind of fairy tale made it worthwhile. And I loved that. I just totally loved that.'

Twirling taffeta dresses and pinstriped suits. We're in the era of Gordon Gecko and Greed Is Good, of Patrick Bateman and Reaganomics. Street crime and the damage caused through the previous decade's recession made the city dangerous. 'I was having problems because dealing with the fear and the crime really affected me,' Danielle says. 'And New York, even at that point in the eighties was super dangerous, people were being shot; I had teachers and student friends that were killed. I was terrified all of the time.'

There were questions in her mind about fashion too. 'I didn't like the industry. I was just doing fashion because I liked creating stuff, but the competition and the trends and the fast-paced living of New York and that ambitiousness and that greed and the power, I didn't like that at all, I liked dreamy things.' Dreaminess floats across Danielle's studio in canvases and vintage furniture and flowers and books. Stacked-up periodicals shimmer across her lilac floor like the ripples of trees across a pond. 'I was always a bookworm,' she says. 'I loved reading about Paris in the twenties, and this brought me to Berlin, because people who were interested in Paris in the twenties were interested in Berlin in the twenties. Brecht, artists during the Weimar, the whole scene here, they were working together and meeting people in Paris, especially in art, but also literature.'

'But Berlin during the eighties, it had a very strange reputation, either you loved or hated it, a lot of people were terrified of it,' she says as she pours tea, dried peonies and orchids lovingly arranged in a vase next to the teapot. 'And people spoke of it as if it were a really drug-riddled, very dark place. New York was dark enough already and I didn't necessarily feel like going to another place just as dark, but it was the year that *Der Himmel über Berlin* was released.' Wim Wenders' film *Der Himmel über Berlin*, or as I'd known it, *Wings Of Desire*, opens in monochrome with an angel in a trench coat, stood high atop a church in Charlottenburg, surrounded by painted clouds. The shot could be from the silent era. We could be watching German expressionism, except for one detail: the angel has an eighties ponytail. 'I wasn't actually interested in going to Berlin,' Danielle says, 'but I saw that movie a week before I came and it showed a different kind of atmosphere than I had ever seen before. It was that kind of forgotten, dreamy, time capsule atmosphere and that really attracted me. It reminded me of the twenties again.'

In the film, the angel falls in love with a trapeze artist and follows her to a concert in a ballroom. When Danielle arrived in Berlin that first time to her friend's loft, Ritterstraße 11, a short walk from Kottbusser Tor, 'it was incredible,' she tells me, 'because all the people in that scene in the movie were going in and out of the apartment.' In that scene, the band Crime and the City Solution were playing. Crime and the City Solution, part of what Danielle calls the Australian sound that ran through bars and clubs and boutiques around Kreuzberg and Schöneberg in the eighties, had undergone various line-up changes and moved a continent since forming a decade earlier. I re-watch this moment again, as the camera pans in mono-chrome across the audience, the faces watching the stage, sway-ing and smoking. The crowd could be from last week, absorbing that Australian sound, epitomised in those few screen minutes as slow-burning tremolo guitars and poetically anguished sing-ing. 'That whole audience was in her apartment,' Danielle remembers, 'it was surreal; it was like the movie was in her loft.'

Der Himmel über Berlin has been described as a symphony to Berlin, and I get this. The camerawork glides spectrally; its movement is light and makes me feel like I'm with the angel as he makes his way across the city. The sound goes further. We hear what the angel hears: the inner thoughts of Berliners, and we hear this weaving in and out of Jürgen Knieper's tran-scendent, often Steve Reichian score. There are echoes now that the filmmakers couldn't have known. Like where the angel wakes up in an utterly different from now Potsdamer Platz. A Potsdamer Platz with a wall running through the middle of it. In these echoes, *Der Himmel über Berlin* becomes a symphony to a Berlin that, as Danielle's partner, Alexander Hacke, has described as no longer existing.

Alexander's studio is directly next door. Both studios sit next to each other, sunk off the studio courtyard like a pair of chalets offset by flowers in bloom. Dimensionally speaking, his is exactly the same as Danielle's, except his interior is filled with instruments. Some of these instruments, such as a large steel cello tucked under the windowsill, remind me of his role in Einstürzende Neubauten. A band he joined when he was fourteen, where objects, often found out of the debris of a still-ruined West Berlin, became repurposed as instruments. Liberated, as Alexander described this process when I had visited his studio. He bowed a long note out of the saw, a sonorous, arched sound like a rusted whale, and he did this elegantly between talking and drinking tea from a Throbbing Gristle mug. The note reminded me of the drones and dark beauty of the couple's collective work as HackeDePicciotto. I write this listening to their album, *The Silver Threshold*, within which, like Danielle's paintings, which take up the side of her studio opposite the books, some hanging, some stacked leaning, there's a dreaminess, but it is a dark dreaminess. Part pagan. Part supernatural. Full of animals and folklore.

When Danielle arrived in Berlin that first time, up all the stairs and into the loft at Ritterstraße 11, 'five people were living there,' she says. 'Roland Wolf, the keyboarder from the Bad Seeds, there was him. Then there was this hairdresser who cut everyone's hair. It was just this huge loft where there were always tonnes of people. The music scene. Neubauten were going in. The art scene. Fashion scene. And they had a little suitcase closet over the bathroom where somebody had been sleeping and had just moved out. I said, "Can I move in?" and they said, "Yeah" and I just ended up staying. I didn't even bother to pick up any of my stuff for about three years.'

'Immediately, I totally felt at home because it had that darkness, but it wasn't the darkness that I felt was dangerous like New York. It was more of a comforting darkness. It was like stepping into a different time. You had the feeling that the city somehow was in touch with the past, more than with the future or with the current. And that was crazy because, in New York, everything is always now or in the future. Not much time is put into thinking about the past; it was almost like stepping into an opposite world.'

'In the loft, Roland introduced me immediately to that whole scene. He played me Diamanda Galás. I hadn't heard much Nick Cave, much Birthday Party. He played all of those things to me; it was like entering into a music lesson of the late seventies, early eighties. He said, "We're going to listen to music now; you don't know enough about music,"' she laughed.

Before New York nightlife, her musical upbringing had been classical; her parents moved around a lot, her dad being in the army, but now she was living in Kreuzberg and there were the sounds of the scene, the sounds of Turkish music along Oranienstraße. No more the smells of chestnuts roasting along Seventh Avenue at dawn, now the smell of fresh-baked bread from the Gay cafe Bierhimmel, a few doors along from the

SO36 club, where the scene would emerge out after another long night into the coal-chugged morning sky. 'Everybody slept till about 3pm,' Danielle remembers. 'You woke up, had a cup of coffee, then you just spent your whole day in cafes, either working or visiting friends. We bought food together but we never really cooked, everybody would just get up and you'd meet immediately. Life was spent in a community.'

One afternoon in the summer, I listened back to our conversation and took a walk west off Kottbusser Tor to find Ritterstraße 11. There was an old guy sitting smoking on the steps of a *Späti* and Turkish kids playing in the sun. A few doors down, there was a renovated *hoff* with the flashy logos of start-up companies on the exterior, and tucked into the *hoff*, a gold-lit cafeteria serving seasonal lunches. When Danielle arrived, her rent was 30 marks, the equivalent of fifteen euros a month. There's a scene in *Der Himmel über Berlin* where the angel has just become a human being and walks in this neighbourhood, along Oranienstraße. This surrounding area is so much of the beating heart of the Berlin I know. Page one on anyone's Berlin starter pack is that this area becomes Kotti, an abbreviation of Kottbusser Tor.

And here's the thing: Kotti isn't just the surrounding area, Kotti is a mood. Some things can be very Kotti. That Automat below Paloma Bar, that's very Kotti. Having a monochrome photo strip taken from that Automat late one night and then pinning it to your fridge is very Kotti. It's interesting to think of Kotti recently being in a country that no longer exists. 'People always say, "How did you do it without a mobile phone?"' Danielle says, drawing back in her chair. I notice the silver logo of Neubauten on her T-shirt. 'But back then, you didn't have to make appointments because you just knew everybody. If you were on a subway, if you were in a cafe, if you went shopping, no matter where you went, you always met a lot of people you knew; it was as if you were in a schoolyard. It'd be like, okay, you want to see someone, they usually hang out in that cafe. You'd go there and they'd definitely one hundred per cent pop up at some point. It was this huge community and you'd hang out and talk about art, talk about philosophy and music, and then you'd plan things together. Everyone was working with everybody.'

The scene that existed together between Kreuzberg and Schöneberg created their own thing. They created their own bars and their own clubs and their own galleries. They had their own independent fashion. And musically, despite the patronage of a few forward-minded souls (Daniel Miller of Mute Records, who released the music of The Bad Seeds being one), they self-recorded and self-released their music. Mostly on cassettes. Paul Hockenos, author of *Berlin Calling*, who I had met that time in Prenzlauer Berg, the one with the American intellectual demeanour and who himself was on the frontline of living through these times, described how that 'if you wanted to, you could duck under in the scene and only deal with the scene. You could be cut off from the rest of the world, even the rest of Berlin.' West Berlin, he describes as 'a subsidised de-industrialised economic basket case.'

One where West Germany's federal government saw this chopped-in-half city, 160 kilometres beyond the political borders of the Western world, as a showcase of the West. Yet one with no industry to speak of. Subsidies helped give reason for people to live in West Berlin. That and waving the conscription to join the West German army. 'A lot of people I knew couldn't name a single regularly employed person to their wider group of friends. Anybody who wanted a career wouldn't come to West Berlin. There were no careers to be made here,' Paul says, mentioning the deep irony, as an aside, that these subsidies attracted a city of radicals and free spirits, perhaps many considering themselves Marxists. Or at least more Marxist than overtly subscribing to Western values, but by their very being in West Berlin, they were manning the frontlines of the Cold War for the West.

'But there were a lot of people that didn't like Berlin back then,' Danielle tells me. 'I had friends that came to visit me and they're like, "Oh my god" because it was a very dark place. It wasn't dangerous, but it was still post-war, pretty destroyed, and very poor. That's why it was so cheap, and it had a wall around it, and you were confronted by the political situation all the time. Which I actually liked because I had the feeling that in comparison to normal where politics are on the head and you don't really see it, let's say, elsewhere in Europe, I had it right in front of my door because I lived right next to the Wall. Every time I went out on the street, I would be confronted with the situation that a Cold War was going on. I liked that, I liked that awareness, but a lot of people couldn't deal with it, a lot of people came and they'd say this is such a depressing city.'

Although they didn't know it at the time, building the Wall could be seen as an unintentional gift from Communist Russia to all artists, free thinkers, radicals and outsiders. In this gift of walling in West Berlin, the USSR acted as ancestral patrons for the conditions inside. A city that, although poor, didn't need amplified hustle to survive, where crime didn't become a factor. 'It felt like the only poor city in the world that as a woman you didn't have to be scared, you could walk around at night. So the art was coming from a place that had no fear at all, in comparison to the New York scene in a state of constant fear, which influenced the music. I got to know the music of Lydia Lunch and Jim Thirwell because they were playing in Berlin, and they were questioning the same thing but they were coming from a really dangerous place. In Berlin, the people were just as poor, but that wasn't dangerous. And that influenced the music in the way that it was dark but it also had humour.' I think of the Dadaesque absurdity at play in the performance group Die Tödliche Doris, whose debut album wasn't afraid to use deliberately funny songs. Or in the absurd juxtapositions of repurposed objects used by Einstürzende Neubauten during the scene era, which often felt like any noise provocation came accompanied by a subtle wink.

'It was interesting that there was a wall because within this wall all borders were trying to be broken or put in question, if there was some kind of "Well, that's the way you have to do it." In Berlin, it would be like, "No you don't, and we're going to do the opposite",' Danielle tells me. I think of Mark Reeder, flaneuring around town proclaiming himself a militarist in old Soviet police uniforms, and how provocative this would have been elsewhere. 'In Berlin, you tried to look different,' she says. 'It was considered very unhip to buy clothes. So everybody would make their own, and everybody would try to look different from each other.

All kinds of barriers were being broken down. For instance, men tried to be non-macho, so they would wear make-up and skirts, and women would try to be especially cool. It was really uncool to be catty; it was considered super embarrassing to be competitive with other women. Women would wear heavy boots and heavy jackets and try to act masculine but in a feminine way. Everything was androgynous. Gender was a very fluid thing. It was very hip to be bisexual, everybody would want to be bisexual, and most people were.'

I ask Danielle, knowing her connection to fashion in these times, when she was making costumes and participating in fashion fares internationally, what was the reaction towards Berliners beyond the wall? 'The Berliners were always considered the crazy people because the stuff that we did was not part of the regular trend. Berliners really were outsiders.'

Danielle and Alex became nomads in 2010. 'A city goes through waves,' she tells me. For years, the couple had become more aware of industry creeping in, commerce, diluting everything that made the city so special. She describes the feeling of entering Berlin as 'anywhere else okay, but not here'. They travelled for eight years, stopping off in places. Each time, noticing the gentrification, the way the roots of separation grew deeper and created more borders. Eventually, they came back. Nowhere else is Berlin. Now, she's noticed more hope, that, she says, 'people are starting to demonstrate more and more, that we need good living spaces and we don't want our city to be destroyed.'

Like in *Der Himmel über Berlin*, recollections of West Berlin in the eighties feel monochrome. Maybe it's that forgotten, dreamy, time capsule-ness Danielle describes. A beautifully strange yet also barren and eerie frontier town beyond the Western world lit up by her new friends, who seemed to both question and reject everything. Yet, in '87 to '89, for those long-termers in the scene, the mood had darkened. 'When I speak to Alex, or I speak to Blixa or Gudrun Gut, who'd been there a lot earlier, they'll say that the last part of the eighties was just horrible,' she says. Speed. Heroin. There were deaths, rituals even. 'They'll tell you it had become too hardcore, drugs had taken over, and that's the difference between me arriving as a New Yorker and the Berliners that had already been experiencing it since the beginning of the eighties, they were all saying, "This can't go on like that, we're all going to die."'

Transition was happening, which would flip a switch from monochrome to colour. I think of the opening scene in *Der Himmel über Berlin* again. When that angel is perched at the crest of that church just off the Ku'Damm. That hollow tooth. I imagine if the angel had stayed an angel just a couple of years longer and been up there, one rainy Saturday afternoon in July, as he listens down to our thoughts, what he may have heard. Would he have heard the liquid chatter between clinking champagne glasses in the nearby KaDeWe? A favourite of the elder ladies of the Ku'Damm, stately and drunk in their hats and gloves, the department store's oyster bar is a scene in itself. But what if he listened further towards Wittenbergplatz, just as the music started? Would he have heard Danielle having a moment of apprehension?

1 July 1989. She had organised this day with her then-boyfriend, Matthias Roeingh. On his birthday, they sent out

invitations and obtained the permit to hold a street gathering. One hundred and fifty people, give or take, had showed up and were waiting around a truck on Wittenbergplatz. 'We didn't know what was going to happen,' she recollects. 'We were really insecure and so we stood around, shuffling.'

Danielle and Matthias had this idea: do a parade. They had a motto: Peace, Joy and Pancakes. And a name: The Love Parade. 'We were both great fans of parades in general, like Rio de Janeiro, and we were always organising parties and fashion shows.' The couple had connected through dancing, where Matthias DJed under the name Dr Motte at the club he co-owned, Turbine Rosenheim, in Schöneberg.

'At the Turbine, they were organising a lot of seventies parties and also in the Gay clubs, that was the thing – seventies parties, disco music, Chic: Dance! Dance! Dance!' This is where Danielle had gotten a bar job. She loved that drink and drugs were never the main ingredients; it was dancing.

'Motte was playing seventies music and then he heard about something new coming in. He started getting the first acid house records and it attracted me because it was so radical.' But, she says: 'Although the passion was there, the music was still very underground.' One night, Matthias came home after DJing and he said to her, 'You know? I've got it! We're going to do our own parade!' Danielle felt an immediate rush of excitement. They sent out invites. One hundred and fifty people came.

'Because dancing on the street was not necessarily hip, a lot of people made fun of us when we invited them,' she tells me. 'And they actually came to look at us and make fun of us because they thought it was so uncool that we were going to do it. They're like, "That's just about the uncoolest thing."' Berlin is (particularly during the late sixties up until the early nineties) a city of demonstrations. The Ku'Damm itself has a particular protest resonance, being where the student leader Rudi Dutschke was shot in the head in 1968 while leaving the office of the Sozialistischer Deutscher Studentenbund, an incident that galvanised the swell of protest. But this, The Love Parade, was about dancing, and that 'we believed that it's important to demonstrate for something rather than against something. Like not to be against things because that will only harden the walls, but to actually try to support good things because that will make new possibilities open up.'

Before the music began, as the crowd shuffled and Danielle twitched, a police officer assigned to oversee the afternoon came over and asked her, 'Well, should we start?' She laughs. 'I had been on my share of demonstrations with Motte, and for a policeman to come up and say, "Shall we start?" felt like such a reversal. And so we said, "Okay." And he said, "Well, what are you going to do?" And we're like, "We're going to turn on the music." And he said, "Well then, do it!"'

At its peak by 1999, The Love Parade had moved a few kilometres to the wide space along the Siegessäule monument, where an estimated 1.5 million people came to dance. That Saturday, a decade before on the genteel Ku'Damm, with its department stores and old-fashioned restaurants, Danielle noticed that it is a lot harder to dance if you're walking than if you're stood still. And that all the people who came just to make fun, who were stood along the sides along with people who were just passing and had stopped to watch, that nobody knew what was happening.

'And this lasted a pretty long time; the music was loud and we were moving to it but it was a little awkward.' After two kilometres, on the turning to Olivaer Platz, 'Motte said, "Okay, let's stop the truck and just dance." And, for me, that's the beginning of what happened after. And you could really feel it. It was this crazy moment which you don't have very often in life, where you suddenly realise that something important is happening. That suddenly, there was a paradigm shift. And all of a sudden, everybody, not only us dancing but people that are watching us, everybody, it was like we had suddenly gone out of our minds.'

Danielle takes a pause. 'And we thought, like a black and white movie, let's bring some technicolour to it. It started raining but actually dancing in the rain was so exhilarating. It was just this epiphany, and those people who laughed at us before and said, "You're crazy, it's not cool, how embarrassing to go and dance down a street", you could just see their jaws drop; everybody's jaws dropped. Ours did and theirs did because everybody felt something happened, something. It was a change of electricity.'

Four months later, the Wall would fall. Like the angel's journey through *Wings of Desire*, Danielle De Picciotto's first years in Berlin saw a transformation that began in black and white and hit a moment that flipped a switch. 'And from that moment on, it never stopped.'

7.

MORNINGS WITH FAYROUZ
FARHAD. SYRIA. OSTKREUZ.

For Farhad, music has always been in his blood, even in the most uncertain times. Hood hanging over cap, he stirs his tea as he reminisces a boyhood, now lost for ever, where family and friends would gather on rooftops overlooking their Damascan neighbourhood. 'I grew up with Syrian traditional music,' he tells me. 'We sometimes used to sleep on the roof. We take our baggies and put them up upstairs and you really felt the freedom. We got somebody who plays the Oud and maybe somebody singing with a good voice and we just sit together.'

One of the thousands that arrived in Germany in 2015 during the height of the refugee crisis, Berlin was an unknown destination, the place most likely of being granted asylum. 'I didn't even know how to get to Germany. I didn't even know how I should start. How it should end. What should I do?' he says, thinking back to the experience he went through as a fifteen-year-old when war reached his neighbourhood and he was forced to leave behind everything. 'I had one backpack. It had water inside. You cannot take clothes with you because if you take clothes with you, they will get dirty and you have no place to change. I hadn't showered for one month, the whole way.'

With all that he's experienced, I find it easy to forget until I see him that he's only in his early twenties. The first time we met, three years ago, he was attending Open Music Lab, an evening school where volunteers, many being name DJs and producers, help train people from marginalised backgrounds, many of whom have experienced being refugees, in production and DJ techniques. At this time, Farhad was nineteen and enthusing about the beats he was making on Ableton and about techno, nothing of the like he'd heard growing up. He was talking about a new genre he wanted to make: Political Techno, crunching 4/4 rhythms and samples of speech about what continues to be happening in his homeland, propulsively conveying messages that he saw getting lost in mainstream media.

Back when the crisis peaked in the news, I was living in London and I remember most of Britain looking away in horror, fed hostility from the tabloids and figures like a pre-Brexit Nigel Farage, just emerging out of his failed Viennese painter phase. However, in Germany, Angela Merkel's government took a different approach, granting asylum to one million people. Concurrently, this didn't stop opposition from the right-wing populist political party, the AFD, and violent responses from neo-Nazi factions. That first time we met, in 2018, three years into his existence as a Berliner, there were nearly 5.6 million registered Syrian refugees worldwide, almost a quarter of Syria's entire pre-civil war population.

It's three years later and we meet up in Ostkreuz Station. Through the spaciously breezy central platform, Farhad emerges, head to toe in white tracksuit, baseball cap tucked under hood. He's maintaining a neat, moustache-less beard, and after we fist-bump, he says, 'Let's go get hot dogs.'

We cut through the concourse towards where he knows a good place. I get a vivid memory of the last time I was here, a Sunday morning on a cold February, leaving the club ://aboutblank, I was with an ex and we stopped to get a cheeky post-club McDonald's, joining a queue along with a bunch of others who'd just left dancefloors. Ostkreuz Station during these hours, located as it is east of Friedrichshain, above Treptower, becomes a dancefloor thoroughfare. ://about blank and Renate are a cigarette's stroll away, a little further blending into the industrial east, Sisyphos and clubs around where the Spree river flows past Rummelsberg, and then it's also just a couple of stops towards Berghain, Kater Blau and Kit Kat, and all those other Spree-side places pumping the city's cultural blood into circulation. Where your average train station at 5am on a Sunday might be a paradise for pigeons and a bench for the homeless, here, clubbers fill across the concourse like department store mannequins in reappropriated nineties sportswear who magically come alive when the normal world sleeps.

Today, though, it's a sunny Friday afternoon, the normal world is awake and we head down Neue Bahnhofstraße, a strip full of loudly decorated eateries reaching out into the road with colourful hoardings. We pull up chairs at the terrace of a restaurant where a DJ booth is being set up along the straße.

Pretty Arabic girls in promotional T-shirts attach helium balloons to the sides of the decks like it's a garden birthday party. Farhad used to flip burgers here but, he says, his heart wasn't into it. However, the staff greet him with familial warmth.

'If you read what is happening in Syria now, it's crazy stuff,' Farhad says, bringing us each a bottled Coke with a straw and sitting down. Right now, his family may be safe from the immediate danger of military fire. Still, like so many regions in a post-war climate that have become vulnerable to corruption, the struggle has just changed form. He explains: 'If you go to the bank and say, "Please save my ten thousand Euros", what's happening is that the bankers are taking that money. When people come to ask for their money, the banks say, "Sorry, we don't have your money anymore." A lot of people lost a lot because the country is sinking in shit.'

A man brings us hot tea. He shakes Farhad's hand enthusiastically. They banter in Arabic and then Farhad introduces me. The man shakes my hand with a vigorous squeeze like an affectionate if over-bearing uncle. After he goes back inside, we quietly laugh at how tight his grip was. Despite Farhad's geniality, he seems tired. He studies at college every morning before working in a shisha bar. He sends half of his wages back to his family every month. When Farhad talks about home, it's of a home that no longer exists, and he talks like someone who loved deeply and lost permanently. Warmth and heartbreak at the same time.

'Everyone lived normally in Syria,' he reflects. 'You have a house, have a family. I think a lot of Germans think that Syrians don't have anything, but my lifestyle was really normal. I'd go to school and my dad would go to work, normal life, you know?' During the long, warm summer evenings, he and his friends would relax on roof terraces, listening to whoever could best play the Oud, whoever could best sing along. Hiding his cigarette smoke from his dad, they'd share jokes about the old men who'd smoke shisha pipes three days straight and then wonder why they'd get mysterious headaches. Farhad's parents would listen to the Lebanese singer Fayrouz in the kitchen and drink coffee every morning. 'And just let it in, you know?' Fayrouz is often described as the Soul of Lebanon. Farhad calls her sound 'wise music, when people listen to her, they think she really knows what I'm in right now.' I confess I don't know her stuff. He tells me she sings about war but keeps the details obscured, that in this way, her songs reach people's hearts rather than widening divides. He glances over my phone as I find her on YouTube. 'I'm advising you to check her out. She has millions of songs, millions of hits. Everyone in Arabic countries love her.'

Life since arriving in Berlin has been about moving forward, facing the unknown. The previous time we met, just before the pandemic, he'd been DJing regularly and told me about playing techno to a room full of older Turkish men at a birthday party. The men were confused, expecting to hear traditional sounds. Right now, he can't produce. He had to sell his Mac, which had Ableton. He did this to help his parents, who've been hit by the ongoing banker corruption. What's fuelling him is UK drill. Dutchavelli, his Notes App, is filling up with rhymes. He tells me that German hip hop is only about girls and guns but not about 'life, the real stuff, like UK drill'. If you can rap well, the money to be made in streams is, his eyes roll, impressive. He does some quick math to demonstrate the profits. There's an entrepreneurial focus to Farhad today. An unnamed mentor has, he tells me, been warming him up to the online business of drop-shipping. The art of distributing goods based around targeted social media ads. The mentor says that if you can invest a year of learning, you can live how you want after twelve months. It's his sixth year now in Berlin but back before, in Damascus, war came to town very quickly. The way Farhad describes it to me, the conflict reached through communities like the tide rolling shore-bound. 'This can happen two weeks or maybe can happen one day,' he recollects the morning that tide reached his neighbourhood. Seeing first-hand 150 troops arriving as he stood by a wall, smoking a cigarette where his father couldn't see him.

'During the war, they offered me money to fight,' he tells me. 'This is how it goes in Syria. So this is how all of these people came out of nowhere in support of America, in support of the European Union. The West just exports weapons. It goes to Syria; they give it to the people and then they get people paid to fight with them. They did the same thing when they took over the part of Damascus I lived in.' He was offered the equivalent of three hundred euros a week to fight. At this time, for one week of this money alone, a person in Damascus could pay rent and buy groceries for several months. 'So they were like, here's your money, now just hold a weapon and go fight. A lot of young Damascans don't live more than a week because they don't know how to fight; they're untrained.'

'I asked my father, what do you think? He said to me, "Do you think you can fight?" I was like, "No, of course not." So he told me: "Just do what you think is right. Do you need money? Just go to work. No need to fight." "Yeah, but no work is not going to give me this much." "Yeah, but go to work, don't get yourself killed because I will not be there when you die." It was tough advice but I needed to hear it. Now, a lot of times before I do anything, I think about what my dad said: Do you think it's right? Do it. Do you think it's not right? Don't do it.'

However, taking this stand created a different kind of danger for Farhad. In not fighting whilst people had signed up, many of whom he knew, he'd isolated himself. A hard decision had to be made quickly. 'So I realised, okay, I'm leaving, I'm not feeling safe here. I couldn't take my parents with me. They didn't want to leave. We had a house, they built it themselves and they knew a lot of families and they all didn't want to leave. I felt sad because I thought it was easy for them to let me go. But it wasn't. On the day I left, my mom cried as shit, but up until then, at that moment, they didn't show anything. They wanted to put their feelings away, so I'd go. They told me, "Right now, you have us, but we don't know what's going to happen. At any point, you might have to rely on yourself." A lot of other friends lost their whole families in the blink of a second.'

At that time, thousands of kilometres north, Merkel's government took the categorically moral decision to open Germany to a million people seeking asylum. 'I don't know anything about Germany,' Farhad he tells me. 'I don't know how to get there. I mean, how the hell do I even find out how to get there illegally? I don't know how I should start, how it should end, what should I do?' And at that moment, our food arrives. I look down and see a hot dog, happy-yellow coloured mustard neatly ducking around the sides of jalapenos tucked into a red plastic bowl. Farhad bites into his burger. I bite into my hotdog. I quickly conclude that this would be a very distasteful time to tell Farhad that I don't eat meat. 'My parents gave me three thousand four hundred euros for the whole way. My dad called some friends, asking them, "My son is getting out, how does he do it?"'

'And then I started. I went from Damascus to Ankara in Turkey.' It was here that he spent the first two weeks preparing for the month-long, 3,700-kilometre journey ahead. 'Because from Turkey, everything starts. You have to look for a smuggler, look for a room, look for everything, and I needed to find somebody to teach me the way. I had to learn quickly how to trust people. I had to learn everything because people get robbed, people drop.' And the first stage facing him was one of the most perilous, the crossing of the Mediterranean Sea to Greece. Farhad found a smuggler that could take him across. 'His name was Tarif. He was quite a cool dude, but . . .', and then, before continuing, Farhad pauses. Over a million migrants took this route that year, often in overcrowded and unstable dinghies. 'But he is smuggling people; he's basically selling people. Tarif told me stories about how people just sink in the sea, but he couldn't help them. That day when he was telling me about that, he was finding this really normal. Maybe he does get sad, but he can't show that because then he thinks maybe I'll get sad too and not want to go on the boat and then not pay the one thousand two hundred euros. Paul, imagine this, you get forty people in a small boat, which costs eight hundred euros. And you get from each one of them one thousand two hundred euros, and they're doing this back and forth. That's really crazy. It's insane. See what I'm saying?'

During 2015, over 2,700 lives were lost at sea. I asked if he felt nervous; after all, he was putting his life in the smuggler's hands. Farhad shrugs. 'Yeah, but I know they just want to reach the Greek islands too.' He gets out Google Maps: 'So, this is Ankara, and somewhere here is Chios islands, where I came in.' Reaching near the shoreline in the dark, he recollects Tarif telling all forty people on the boat to jump overboard and swim towards red lights. Red lights meant land and, reaching land, the group of forty would stick together for most of the journey.

Their timing was lucky. In March 2016, the EU–Turkey Deal was made, which essentially meant that every person arriving at the Greek islands without official permission would be returned to Turkey. Borders were shutting down. If Farhad had left merely months later, his whole life in Berlin may well never have happened. In Ankara, the group were given a three-day period of grace to pass through and reach Bulgaria. He tells me that to do this, the group had to do something that, to me, feels utterly counterintuitive. 'You go to this police station,' he says. 'You say, "Yeah, I'm here, I'm a refugee, I just need a place to sleep." You stay there two, two and a half days and then the police gave you a paper to leave Greece.'

The paper allowed the group to take a train to Bulgaria, where they had to find and pay a smuggler five hundred euros to guide them on foot to Macedonia. 'Here, I started to use

Google Maps and we put the walk into the borders. It was four hours, but we could not smoke cigarettes because of the light. No foods. Just check your phone and keep going. I had one backpack, that's it.' He says this and we've finished eating a while ago and we're now drinking tea. I tell him what he just said brings up one of the crudest misconceptions less sympathetic voices across Europe used against people experiencing being a refugee. Dirt. Being in England in 2015, I remember this narrative. In July, Prime Minister David Cameron described migrants as 'swarms of people coming across the Mediterranean'.

This was not new. Three years prior, New Labour Home Secretary David Blunkett referred to child asylum seekers as 'swamping' British schools. This manipulation of language, harmful enough as it is, became ammunition for the right-wing press to amp up and stir a disenfranchised society finding a nascent Brexit voice. As if by letting these people enter our country, they'll infect our ways. 'Exactly!' Farhad slams. 'Like imagine when we were walking the borders, we had to walk on the highway and thousands of cars were watching us but I don't give a shit about that because I can't go back,' he says. 'If I give a shit that everyone looks at me, oh man, I'm just not going to go on. I'm just gonna stop and see if somebody helps me. Maybe I would last two or three months maximum and then my money runs out. No papers, so I can't work. It's going to end badly. So I just had to carry on – it was winter, raining, highway, cold, fuck it, let's do it. Just keep going.'

They kept going, and it was towards the final stretch, travelling through Austria in cars, that intolerance, fear, whatever you want to call it, almost caught up with the group. 'So from Belgrade, you call a smuggler and pay him seven or eight hundred euros to get you a car, a private car, like BMW, Mercedes. Any car, so that when you cross the borders in a car, nobody questions you.' The group pulled in at a busy Markt Hall, as Farhad passed along stalls selling cheese, vegetables, a variety of German meat and flowers to a kiosk where he could buy water. He clocked a thick tension in people's behaviour. There were police; they had arrested an African refugee.

'This motherfucker working in a shop,' Farhad spits, 'she asked to see his ID for cigarettes. He didn't have this; she picked up on that he was dirty, so she called the cops.' The contempt in Farhad's voice for this woman quivers out of his throat like a fresh wound. It's the only point in the times we've hung out that I see him angry. Suddenly, there's a burst of sound, an electrical noise like a cable yanked out of an amp. The pretty girls in promotional T-shirts, people on benches eating burgers and hot dogs, a technical looking person wiring the decks close by us, and us too, we all jolt. Jolted out of one moment, into another. Farhad and I share a sad laugh and then the wound is gone from his face. There are moments, like the very final stages of his route, a train from Munich to Berlin, he tells me in such a calm, blunted voice, it's like he could be handing me down a series of instructions in case someday I might need to do this myself.

Meanwhile, 'We can do it!' were Merkel's famous words, and Germany began the task of processing one million new arrivals. For the next sixteen months, whilst the administration filtered its way through to reach Farhad, he lived in a hastily repurposed hostel in Mitte. I go to find it one morning in early September. The view of the Fernsehturm, that giant tower, once a monument of GDR power, now a compass, darts in and out of the buildings along Torstraße as I cycle. Sometimes in Berlin, when the sky is heavy the air cloaks the Fernsehturm and the entire monument can seem to disappear altogether before reappearing closer than anticipated like a boat through the fog. Just as Torstraße veers uphill north on one side towards Prenzlauer Berg and downwards on the right to Friedrichshain, I find the hostel. Closed. Permanently. Bird shit around the entrance. To its left, a graffiti-tagged yellow ATM and an app-based rent-a-bike rack system, and nobody has taken away the purple sign saying Pangea People Hostel that hangs above the bolted-up doorway. Berlin is constantly in metamorphosis yet always leaving traces of the past. During the height of the crisis, camps in sports halls and aircraft hangers became over-populated, asylum-seekers and volunteers lived and worked in harsh living conditions, struggling with poor supplies. Yet, in Pangea People Hostel, Farhad tells me he was luckier than many. 'The people who worked there, they were kind,' he says. 'They showed me the real meaning of health and love when I was sixteen years old, when I was alone and my family wasn't with me. They made it feel my second home.'

He even went back to visit the staff, unaware that in the time since he'd left, Pangea People Hostel had closed. He shared his dorm with eight others, Arabs, Africans and Argentinians, detained and given one euro a day each to live on. 'So you can't do anything except eating and sleeping. You play with your phone or go to the upstairs bar or the computer rooms.'

It's weird to think that during this time, on a visit to the city, a couple of years before becoming a resident myself, I might well have been just across the road in Soho House, sipping mojitos with fresh mint, ordering a side plate of shishito peppers with a miso glaze, lured into relax mode via a journeying DJ playing tried and tested lounge house. It was in the computer rooms at Pangea that he met Suzy, a volunteer. 'She had her shift until 8pm and then after, she doesn't get paid for it but she'd teach us German. Like every day, two or three hours until we actually started speaking a little bit. One day, when Suzy finished teaching us, somebody asked, "What are you doing after?" and Suzy said, "I'm going with some friends to the club." "Ah okay, what kind of club? What kind of music?" I ask. "Techno." "Techno? What is that?" "I cannot tell you. You have to hear it for yourself, but you cannot go to the club because you're too young",' Farhad laughs. 'Well, I was sixteen and I got curious. A few weeks after, we were in a computer room where they had good speakers and she showed me a video of DJ Stingray, the one who wears a mask. It was a whole new something new for me. I mean, I don't even know how to dance to it. I didn't even understand what kind of music it was at first. I was just wondering why the whole thing is the same and why there's only one kick drum. Why is this? She just said it's powerful.'

Up until then, Farhad only listened to Arabic music, every morning back in Damascus the strings and sentiments of Fayrouz, the nights with Oud on the roof. But now, a seed was set. DJ Stingray, Redshape, this unfamiliar, initially perplexing sound that Suzy opened the gateway to grew over the next six months in the computer room. Headphones and streaming.

Boiler Room. Ben Klock. Another click. VTSS. Another link. Further in. SoundCloud. Clicking further. Berghain line-ups, then scouring releases on Ostgut. That kick drum, initially so blank, now a pulse guiding Farhad deeper. Along the way, new variations. New textures. Acid. House. Breakbeat. Drum & Bass.

Farhad lights a cigarette and offers me one. I decline; daytime smoking makes me feel dizzy. 'You mean just cigarettes?' He finds this funny. The smoking, the drinking, in doing so, he knows he's not representing his faith. 'This is why sometimes I feel depressed. Maybe because I forgot God, that's why God forgot me,' he told me the previous time we hung out, a bitterly cold November evening near Checkpoint Charlie where, over warm Turkish tea in a cafe, he still felt sadness for having lost his phone on his journey here. 'I recorded the whole way. The whole way.'

Memories, photos. 'I had pictures in every place, in every city, but the phone is gone, the police in Macedonia took it. This is the thing I'm most sad about.' He sees clearly now that at that time we met near Checkpoint Charlie, he was deep in a period of existential questioning. We've lived through a pandemic since then, and today, something has shifted. He has his own place in the outer-ring suburb Schöneweider, studies, works, gets home, lights a joint and watches a movie. Right now, there is no Mac, no Ableton, just iNotes, UK drill and the rhymes of Dutchavelli. Yet he's proud. The money for selling that music gear paid for rent and food for his parents. I mutter, 'So, you're the breadwinner.'

I always forget that my English expressions can seem oblique in Berlin, but 'breadwinner' makes him laugh and, for the first time, I see how literal an expression it is. 'There are people like me who have to send money to their families in Syria, but unlike me, they do not have papers, so they can't get a job, so what can they do? They have to sell drugs, or they steal. They cannot do anything about it; if they didn't steal or sell drugs, they would not live and they wouldn't be able to send money home.'

We talk about the African dealers in Görlitzer Park. 'If you don't have any papers and you're not allowed to work, what can you do? I have a lot of friends from these people. They help me in my bad days.' In his bad days, depression arises; he's sensitive to negative energy, particularly those energies of people he serves during long work shifts, customers who like things just so. Westerners, particularly Germans, he confesses, can be cold. We abandon our families and project our stress on service staff. 'My mom got sick and I couldn't send her money,' he says. 'And this one friend, I can never forget him, he sells his phone to get my mom's medicine. He said to me, "This is for all our mothers."' More recently, his mother helped him reconnect with the faith he'd been questioning over a series of phone conversations. 'Back in Damascus, I used to go out with friends at night, but I also prayed to my God. Takes you five minutes. Five times a day, five minutes and that's it. Do it. Just do your duty.'

The late afternoon sun beats down on the awning. That intangible energy that here has its own word but we have no satisfying English translation for, *Feierabend*, is happening. You can feel it in the flow of movement around us. The pink helium balloons attached around the decks feel it, jolting as they are in confused airstreams as the straße fills with people jumping into whatever the weekend means to them. In English, we might call this knocking-off time. This is inaccurate, a German is likely to respond. *Feierabend* energy is concentrated, swelled up in a strip like this, Neue Bahnhofstraße, a thoroughfare to an even larger thoroughfare.

Maybe the decks feel it too, or at least maybe they will once a DJ starts playing on them. The DJ in me wonders what music I would play to sell hot dogs on a Friday evening in Ostkreuz. Farhad runs inside to settle up. Like that time near Checkpoint Charlie, he absolutely insists on paying for everything. I think if we ever meet again, he will insist on paying that time too. I think of the hot dog I ate. I'd not eaten meat in years. I didn't feel bad but I wondered for a second if I'd now awoken my inner carnivore, who'd now threaten mutiny the next time I'm picking vegan schnitzel out of the Lidl freezer cabinet.

We're back on the concourse of Ostkreuz Station; we're talking about what each of us is going to do over the weekend. Both our plans seem equally vague. Suddenly his train arrives, and we briefly fist-pump before Farhad disappears into the bustling carriage. Train doors close.

Something he said three years ago when we first met rings in my head. Later I will find this quote. 'When I came from Syria, there were a lot of borders to cross, a lot of things you have to do to just represent who you are. Here in Berlin, I don't feel any borders; it's connected feelings. You are a musician; you are welcome here.' Back then, in the summer of 2018, he was a student at Open Music Lab, under tutorage from DJs that you will probably know but I will not name here, as befits the selfless intentions of volunteer work. He was getting to grips with Ableton and making Political Techno. He came bouncing into the classroom that day, a puppy, wanting to tell me all about what making beats meant to him. This unexpected way of connecting through one kick drum in a new city in a country he knew nothing about. He was borrowing equipment and coming into the studio out of hours. Life since arriving in Berlin has been about moving forward, facing the unknown. I feel sad that he's not making beats, but I question if this is fair for me to feel this way. After all, he's a son that any Western parents could only dream of.

Suddenly, I reach my bike, chained up on a railing underneath Ostkreuz Station, and have a moment where I feel like I've turned into Emily In Paris. My parents are getting older. I briefly wonder if I'll pass a *Sparkasse* on the cycle home, so I won't get charged a transaction fee, but then I forget.

8.

CAPTAIN MARVEL JR IN BERLIN

ALAN OLDHAM. DETROIT. PRENZLAUER BERG. RADIO. SCI-FI. CREATION.

'You were there?' Alan Oldham sounds surprised, modest even. I've just mentioned the first time I experienced him DJing. It was at a snug, low-lit bar on Greifswalder Straße. The bar's name hangs above bottles of spirits and lacquers in electric blue neon. It's the name of a piece of music by New York proto-punks Suicide, which happens to be the bar manager, Andrew's favourite song: Dream Baby Dream. Below the neon, there are always a couple of beautiful people dressed in neat black, slicing limes, shaking ice. They know all of their locals, of which, for quite some time, I was one. The DJ booth is squeezed into a couple of metres of space between where the bar ends and a window begins. Well, when I say DJ booth, I mean a hefty oak table with CDJs, a mixer, some cocktails and most likely an ashtray overspilling, if not from the DJ playing then from where an elegantly arched hand of a patron might reach across from their bar-side position.

Alan's surprise, I think, isn't at all down to the bar's low-key atmospherics. Dream Baby Dream is hardly the large furnace of Tresor, to which Alan maintains a status of unofficial resident. After all, he has been in the neighbourhood for some years now. Neither does his surprise carry any egoic notion of stature that I should catch a one-time member of Underground Resistance and the first radio DJ in Detroit to play the emerging hard sci-fi of The Belleville Three in a cocktail bar in Prenzlauer Berg. A cocktail bar small enough that the aroma of fresh basil being cut behind the bar greets you upon entrance. And one where if you ask nicely, the DJ usually lets you stash your coats and bags underneath the oak booth.

'I'm shocked that you were there,' Alan laughs. In this conversation, supposed to be about Detroit and Berlin and techno and the role this most unassuming of gentlemen played in it, his surprise, I'd hazard a guess, has nothing to do with Dream Baby Dream and everything to do with what he was playing. But there he was, behind those squeezed-in decks, a tram running across the outside of the window, wearing a T-shirt saying, 'I'm Not Carl Cox', rocking out minutes into 'Leave Them All Behind' by Ride. Wall of noise guitars, fragile Byrdsian harmonies, crashing nineties drums, all eight minutes of it.

My friend and I sipped cocktails, we ordered something with citrus, plum and mezcal, named after one of their own resident DJs – The Brvtalist. Next, Alan played 'Only Shallow' by My Bloody Valentine and, through the bar's speakers, those lost harmonies that sound like Karen Carpenter beamed off the moon sent a chemical reaction running down my spine. It was that week between Christmas and New Year's Eve. That week where people go to their families and nobody is about and my friend and I were not with our families. I heard someone once describe this week as the perineum, the name given to the area on the human body between the anus and the genitals. And on the way to Dream Baby Dream, we weren't even sure if it'd be open. But for the next hour, we sat, hardly talking, sipping and feeling rushes, smiling at each other, at the beautiful people making drinks. At Alan, who grinned and slammed, modestly, to Curve, to Slowdive. Shoegaze music made in Britain in the very early 1990s and, initially, a stark contrast for what you might assume somebody with a techno legacy nearly as old as techno itself to play.

'Well, there again, we have to go back to the early nineties. It was the full-on wannabe musician experience back in those days,' Alan says, thinking back to a time in Detroit when he was balancing his radio show with working three days a week in a record shop. 'And this was when that first wave of shoegaze stuff started coming across to America. Curve, My Bloody Valentine and Slowdive. Those were the three original shoegaze bands that came over, at least to where I was able to hear them.' We're having this conversation through Zoom, where Alan is framed in front of a pine mezzanine several kilometres north of where I am. Pandemic precautions. 'I loved Curve right away because they had the dance beats under their thing, but My Bloody Valentine, that was a bomb going off. There are so many bands that are still chasing that sound but back in those days, you just put your headphones on and lay back and listen.'

We're nearing the end of this conversation; it's nearly two years after my friend and I had shared these hours inside Dream Baby Dream. That very week the government in Wuhan confirmed they were treating dozens of cases of pneumonia of an unknown cause. You always think – would I have gone out more? Would I have hugged every person? I'd never even bought hand sanitiser. I almost didn't ask him about this night; it was an aside I thought I'd just throw in. Still, now Alan's cottoned on that I'm a genuine appreciator. We've suddenly become just two fellow nerds sharing memories told through nineties records.

'So, on a side note, when I was in Underground Resistance and I was going on tour with Mike Banks, and at that time Creation Records had an electronic offshoot label called Infonet,' Alan, the collector, the enthusiast, tells me, 'everybody wanted a UR record. All these different A&R guys were trying to court Mike, you know, "Come with us, do a record with us."' At this time, Creation Records was, despite the transcendental drone-like qualities of My Bloody Valentine and Ride, as well as the cool indie kid scenester embrace of acid house that was Primal Scream's *Screamadelica*, primarily known as a jangly indie guitar label. 'Long story short,' Alan says, 'we visited Creation when we were in London. We went into their offices and I actually met Alan McGee.'

A vocal sample that triggers across the soulful, melodic strings and raw, dry machinic funk of one of Underground Resistance's first tracks, 'The Theory', runs: 'The needs of the many outweigh the needs of the few.' The following sample describes 'molecular structure being reorganised at the subatomic level'. Marxism and science fiction. Formed by 'Mad' Mike Banks, Robert Hood and Jeff Mills, UR sought to offer inner-city African-American youth alternative identities through political action and an alternative sci-fi utopia accessible through machines. Alan had been settling into the collective's Minister of Information role, co-ordinating PR through fax machines. Then in '92, he replaced Jeff Mills as a live DJ, taking the moniker DJ T-1000 after the unstoppable liquid metal cop from *Terminator 2*. Creation were amongst the labels eager to release something by this most politicised, urgent Detroit collective, possibly wanting their own Kraftwerk meets Public Enemy.

'All Mike knew was that these guys wanted to sign Underground Resistance, but I walk in the office and there's fucking posters on the wall: Jesus and Mary Chain, Slowdive. I was like, "Fuck."' We're both laughing, but before we get back on track, I just have to tell him that I, too, was once inside that same building. The Creation offices, just to the side of the overground rail bridge, before Westgate Street in Hackney rolls over into London Fields. That era I lived as an East Londoner and Creation Records was long gone in that era. Instead, a green shop sign said Benmax above a non-existent doorway. I found myself at a house party there. We'd raided drinks in a kitchen that felt like a student houseshare and we kept Julio Bashmore's 'Au Serve' on repeat. I don't think any of us had the faintest idea that so many pieces of music from the early nineties went through this building. Music nerds we may be, but when a piece of music someone plays opens a realm that immediately transports you to another time and reminds you who you were dating, where you were sleeping, what your favourite shirt was, all time converges.

Alan's Instagram bio as I write: DJ T-1000. Black Man From The Future. Detroiter. Berliner. Expat. Artist. Producer. WAV Jockey. Komik Zeichner. Influencer since before the internet. I review a recent set of his on the Berlin streaming station, Hör Radio. The cam shows Alan, framed inside the yellow toilet-like room that is the station's booth. The booth itself, tucked amid an *Altbau* just minutes' walk from the ravers who dance between trees and dealers who sell weed in Hasenheide Park.

Alan wears another of his white-font-on-black-cut T-shirts; this one says, 'Detroit Hustles Harder'. He begins with one of his own, a DJ T-1000 cut; it's called 'I Fucking Love Berlin'. I estimate it's travelling at 145bpm. Stripped down and even a little bolshy, the track, like Alan, has travelled through four decades of techno that have seen that early soulful utopianism of synth strings and melody become submerged somewhere along the way. Instead, I'm transported into those dimensions that trance-based sound can take you into via the processes achievable through digital audio workstations: little dubbed-out loops and fragments that run low in the mix. Utopian worlds themselves, living in the shadows. Alan fucking loves Berlin. Back in 1995, twenty years before he'd move here full time, Alan set his foot down off the plane at Tegel Airport. At the time, he'd started a label, Generator, and was on tour with Mike Banks.

He'd been invited to play Mayday. That day on 1 May when all of Kreuzberg, SO36, turns into a street party: a web of sound systems, generators, protestors and punks, ravers and regulars. 'It was me, WestBam and Luke Slater, and they called me out of the blue. In those days, you put your records out and your phone number was on them. That's how you used to get gigs.' However, any feel for the city was lost in the tour schedule. 'It was one of those things where you arrive at the airport; it's night. You go to the hotel, sleep, wake up, it's dark. Go and play the gig; it's dark. Leave early in the morning, 5am. You're back on the plane and didn't see anything.'

Alan fucking loves Berlin. He talks to me about the creativity, the sense of being able to be himself, of leaving the house and always meeting like-minded people. About the family of souls he became part of through Tresor. Of how he couldn't be making a living the way he does here anywhere else in the world, where, running alongside music, he's an illustrator and comic book artist. 'Corn from Underground Resistance, Cornelius Harris, like me he's also a comic book fan. He used to work at a comic book shop years ago,' he says. 'And we were talking about Berlin and he asked me the same as you: what made me come here full time? Here's my analogy. You're newsboy Freddy Freeman, and your leg is busted. You walk with a limp and you have a crutch, but if you say Captain Marvel, you turn into Captain Marvel Jr and you are a young superhero and you are perfect. When I'm in America, I'm Freddy Freeman, but I say the magic word, I come to Europe and I'm fucking Captain Marvel Jr and I can fly and I'm bulletproof and I'm perfect.' Alan laughs deep. 'So here I am, I'm captain Marvel Jr in Berlin and I'm nobody in America.'

Alan was born in 1963 in Northwest Detroit and grew up in a city both synonymous with music and car manufacture. 'Many of my uncles worked at the plants. Ford, Chrysler, Kelsey-Hayes. It was the golden age of the Black middle class,' he says. The city still produces the most American-made vehicles and is said to employ two-thirds of the industry's autoworkers. Before the recession that would decimate across the city during the early sixties, car production was a lifeblood. Detroit's Motown, itself a play on Motor City, borrowed the industrial assembly line techniques of the car plants: writers working on compositions, passing them on to the session musicians, passing on to singers. Every individual component of a Motown record assembled to become part of a unified machine.

Later, in his twenties, Alan was at college majoring in Radio, TV and Film. He had intentions to become a radio presenter, then a friend told him a local radio station was looking for a summer intern. 'And the studio was located right near my campus. I didn't have a car, so I basically marched up in there and they pretty much gave it to me on the spot.' WDET is part of NPR, the nationwide body of over a thousand regional stations. 'So, to put it in context, this is when *Graceland* by Paul Simon was out, 1987–88. And because of that album, world music was really big, a lot of African music, Caribbean music.' Across in the library of WDET, Alan was given his first project. 'I spent the summer alphabetising the whole library because it was just a mess. Everybody just threw stuff anywhere. And I learned a lot about music during that summer because while I was alphabetising, I was listening. There were special shows on the air; you had a bluegrass show, you had a jazz guy, you had a reggae guy, so on and so forth. Long story short, the overnight guy ends up getting fired. Why? I don't know.' The program director asked Alan if he had a tape, which he did, and if so, if he'd be interested in taking over his slot, which he was. He called the show Fast Forward and it ran on the graveyard shift, three to six. 'I had done some artwork for Derrick May for his Transmat label. And he gave me a bunch of records to play. He said, "Oh man, you got a radio show, that's cool, here man, play these." And these were white labels of the very first Detroit techno records. I was playing Detroit techno, Chicago house. So you figure, this is 1987, it was at this point in musical history, in my music history, where electronic body music was coming from Europe. This is where you started having Front 242 and Thrill Kill Kult, the Belgian stuff, Lords of Acid. And you had acid house in the UK, you had Chicago house, Trax Records. And then you had Detroit techno all at once.'

'My original show was a mishmash of everything, because also I still liked jazz fusion from the seventies, and then there was all these promos the radio station was getting that nobody was playing. All the Cabaret Voltaire stuff, all Kraftwerk, anything that was on Wax Trax!, which is like Front 242 and Ministry.' Those early techno white labels that stemmed out of Juan Atkins, Kevin Saunderson and Derrick May. Like Alan, the three young producers who also drew deep into the power of sci-fi and, named after the suburb they grew up in, became known as The Belleville Three would be beamed across NPR. 'I was getting all that music and there was no outlet at the time to be playing it until I came along.' The differing energies between different cities: Detroit and Chicago. 'I always felt that the Detroit sound, in general, was more aggressive than Chicago and that's kind of why I liked it. The Chicago stuff was soulful. It had a lot of churchy vocals, Byron Stingily, the Frankie Knuckles touch, and everything was really deep. But then when you got to Detroit, man, you had banging stuff, like old Kevin Saunderson, the Reese, and Santonio Kevin Saunderson not the Inner City Kevin Saunderson. You had Derrick's original stuff, Juan's stuff, and Juan's stuff had that heavy sci-fi thing to it. What always differentiated Chicago and Detroit for me was that the Detroit stuff was more aggressive and more forward-thinking. It was based in futurism and sci-fi, just black nerds imagining something else.'

Just black nerds imagining something else. 'We were Afrofuturists and we still are,' Alan says, 'and that's what I liked about Detroit techno, and as far as my artwork's concerned, all this stuff went into my sensibilities.' Sci-fi runs through the origins of techno: Juan Atkins as Model 500's N'o UFOs' from 1985. Echoed vocals about UFOs flying on the cusp of acid house. Back, back further. Right back into years before I even knew techno existed. Somewhere morphing out of electro by way of a bedroom in Belleville, 'Cosmic Cars' by Cybotron (Cybotron being Juan Atkins again, this time with 3070). Go back and YouTube it, unless you're someone extortionately lucky to own the vinyl. 'Cosmic Cars' details leaving behind the surrounding reality in a cosmic car, literally transforming Detroit's industrial product into a sci-fi escape capsule: 'I wish I could escape from this crazy place,' sings a staccato voice.

Imagining something else. The Afrofuturist author Ytasha Womack has described Afrofuturism as the intersection between black culture, liberation and the imagination. I think too of *Mothership Connection*, a psychedelic UFO that arrived out of the Detroit skyline in the late sixties, where soul met rock under the eminence of George Clinton, a one-time Motown session musician. Recreating himself in pseudonyms like Dr Funkenstein and calling his music Clone funk, the sleeve artwork for Funkadelic's *Standing on the Verge of Getting It On* is an Afrofuturist comic book world in itself. This something else runs through Alan's work as a comic book illustrator and sleeve designer, dating right back to comics he'd make with his best friends at school: fifteen issues of the hand-drawn *Crusaders Seven*, where they'd fight villains such as the nefarious Spirit of Detroit. Alan's art draws on a rich lexicon of cyborgs, industrial futurism and sassy heroines with names like Orietta St. Cloud. Some of them, it's not hard to imagine bursting out of the page and jumping behind the DJ booth. When I see these heroes, I can see Schöneberg-raised legend Ellen Allien, herself both sci-fi hybrid and part of Mitte's scenery. Alan, coincidentally, is part of her BPitch Control label.

Now the synthetic strings, sci-fi captions and robotised funk rhythms are largely gone, and Berlin has long since created so many of its homegrown techno identities that I sometimes wonder if this city gives its due to the legacy of Detroit. Alan feels so. 'And that's another one of the reasons why I like it here,' he says. 'A lot of credit for that has to go to Dimitri Hegermann because he is the guy more than anyone who pushed the Detroit–Berlin connection.' Hegermann's Tresor, established in its original location in vaults under the abandoned Wertheim department store thirty years before this conversation, when the surrounding area, Potsdamer Platz, was still a post-war wasteland and utterly unrecognisable from the characterless shopping mall of now. Tresor's forward motion: to play music harder, faster and darker than in the warehouses and emerging clubs elsewhere. 'Dimitri was one of the first guys to bring Detroit guys here, the guy that brought Underground Resistance to Berlin for the first time. And it was this historical nexus where you had early Detroit techno, the fall of the Wall, and you had this whole new youth culture here in Berlin all at the same time.' People talk about that first Tresor as if it was a furnace with intense heat and thick walls. 'The techno was 140bpm and up, and Tresor was this closed space,' Alan recollects. 'It was super hot, the ceiling was dripping and you were still playing vinyl back then. You had sweat and condensation on the records and you had to kind of do something like this' – he mimes wiping a record with a cloth – 'while you played to keep everything from coming down. And you would leave there, you'd blow your nose and out would come all this dust and black shit.'

'I think that Detroit, Chicago and New York are given their proper due here because the things that I do are considered serious and cultural. Because I'm not just DJing to a bunch of people on drugs, this is actual culture. I can make a living here doing what I do. It's taken seriously and that's what I appreciate. I couldn't make a living doing what I do in the States. If it's not a corporate paycheque, they don't take it serious.'

Imagining something else. Over thirty years later, people draw on what was imagined in Detroit to maintain a reality in Berlin. 'I can't think of another place where culture is still held as being the life force,' Alan says. Whether you want to grasp it or not, Berlin is an outpost. It may not be in the literal sense of a pre-'89 walled-in West Berlin. You can spend evenings debating whether, in a stadt gridded up with start-up investment and where beloved free outposts like Kunsthaus Tacheles are being ripped into expensive apartments, it is still the free, wild and creative outpost it once was. But maybe that makes that something else imagined even more worth saving.

'That's why I got involved in this initiative,' Alan says. Currently, he's become active in a campaign by Rave the Planet formed by Dr Motte to lobby German authorities to apply for UNESCO's Intangible Cultural Heritage. 'Clubs like Tresor with a long history can be protected as cultural sites. And therefore, you're protected from gentrification and more condos that nobody can afford. Gentrification is creeping in really fast, and we do have to protect this thing.' Alan believes too that the initiative can be adapted for Detroit. 'Because so much music and culture that comes from Detroit remains unrecognised, in my opinion. Other cities are known as music cities. You go to Nashville; you go to Memphis and Sun studios. But somehow, Detroit gets the murder capital democratic hell hole . . . for some strange reason which I just can't understand.'

He says that last sentence very slowly and very deliberately. The meaning is unambiguous. 'And then when you go back and see just the sheer talent that's come from Detroit and not just techno, but in every genre of music.' He namechecks other Detroit natives – Iggy and the Stooges. The MC5. Patti Smith. Motown. George Clinton's axis of psychedelia. Bob Seger. Aaliyah. Eminem. 'I mean, come on, man, it's a great city and it should be protected.'

9.

BEYOND THE LINE

JULIA. SONIA. BERGHAIN. THE SNAKE. INSIDE. SAFER SPACES.

'Before I go to Berghain,' Julia says, 'I always ask myself, why am I going? Am I trying to escape, or do I want to gain something from it to take back into life?'

When the day finally came, she wasn't even sure if she wanted to go; she'd been feeling sick all week, the tests said negative; she knew instinctively it was just the change of the seasons, but for all the uncertainties and closures of the last nineteen months, this is the thing she missed the most. She has her routine. Her favourite place inside. Her personal sweet spot. But now the day had come and Julia was questioning: 'Am I really this fan girl who needs to be there the day it opens?'

Julia tried to recreate the feeling at home, particularly in the early months when nobody knew what the fuck. Headphones on, re-arranging the lights, dancing in her studio up high near Tempelhofer Feld. She regretted not going that last weekend back in March 2020. That last weekend when people had already started debating whether or not they should be going out. But she's danced. She's danced since in open air in festivals across Germany. Those biergartens though: the idea of sitting down, just listening, mask strap on arm like a ghoulish wristband, unable to dance, sounded like torture. For Julia, there are things about Berghain she feels are wrong, the way internal inclusivity is matched by external exclusivity, for one, and as much as she's tried, she's kept open to the potential of finding an alternative elsewhere. But. Nothing. Comes. Close.

She considered staying in, having an early night. 'But then I thought: if this place exists again and it's open and people are dancing and I'm not there, I won't be able to go to sleep anyways,' Julia tells me. We're in the kitchen of her shared workspace; there is a big white room opposite that she uses as a photographic studio. I first met her through photography, when she was an assistant on a shoot and I had agreed to model for a friend. For the shoot, in a Kreuzberg Airbnb filled up with props, the glare of camera lights and crew, I was naked and I agreed to have my penis painted blue to match the colour of Steph the photographer's electric blue canary. Julia hadn't long moved from Hamburg and was building up connections in the city. Someone found a stack of vinyl and had put on The Velvet Underground and Nico, and Julia, pink hair and fringe like she has now, asked me if I'd like a tea. Not just any tea but an English tea. Kink and comfort together in that moment.

She was late in discovering Berghain; she jokes that this is typical of her, late with everything. Yes, she visited Berlin a few times as a teenager on vacation, but then those experiences are always different, based in tagging along, somebody always keeping an itinerary dangling like an umbilical cord to home that stops you having time and space to fully let go. Into her early twenties, her interest in electronic music had been growing steadily, but when she got to hear about Berghain, wasn't it all just hype? It's like whatever transcendence you might find on the inside, whatever bonds and new family wait, whatever personal revelations all seem to evaporate like smoke when you try to explain it on the outside. Berghain becomes hyperbole. Meme account. Jokes about wearing black. Context-free descriptions of sexuality. Plus, she felt, if Berghain has such a tough door policy, why the fuck would they let her in?

That first time, she got the train from Hamburg, staying with a friend who'd cared to prepare her way in. 'He made a whole production out of it,' she says. 'The week before he was sending me sets of the DJs going to play, he was sending me pictures of examples of what people wear, he was saying, "Well, my girlfriend usually wears something like this or like this."' She remembers seeing the building for the first time, the line moving quickly, seeing Sven at the doorway and that moment where he looks at you, his mind already made up, and god it must be so easy for him to clock people's energies once the line takes you into that final cow-grid. It's in the cow-grid where she really starts to feel the rattle of the Ostgut sound. The kick drum from inside radiating across all the metal on the outside. Sven nodded and they were in. 'And it took me a couple of hours, then I started to feel so at home,' Julia says. 'I asked my friend if he thought anyone minds if I take off my pants and my shirt? And he said, "Look around, you can do whatever you want here."' Yes, she danced during the pandemic, but there was always something just not quite right. Maybe the people, maybe the sound, maybe the way the space was organised, maybe the music. All equal ingredients, and although different tastes may sip to different recipes, for Julia, elsewhere was never quite right. And that's not without trying, the concept of being dependent on one place an anathema to the open-minded. When we first met through the glare of the camera lights and she had made me feel so comfortable, we bonded in chat about recent moments we'd had travelling east in Europe. I'd been to Kyiv and danced in Closer, where Helena Hauff had played a set of acid, and she'd been to Tbilisi, but for her, it always came back to Berghain. 'After that first weekend,' she said laughing, 'this was the final push I needed to move to Berlin.'

It's 2 October 2021. That giant banner that hung down from the top, visible across the surrounding industrial scrubland, the banner that asked *Morgen Ist Die Frage*, has been taken down, Tomorrow Is the Question has been clarified on wristbands: *Musik Ist Die Antwort*. Tonight, this big old transmitter, *The Big House*, as a friend calls it, is reopening. During the pandemic, the building wasn't entirely out of use. Weekend garden parties and midweek outdoor events had been happening since July, and there was also the time it reinvented itself temporarily as a gallery. A logical transformation. For one, the aforementioned bouncer Sven Marquardt has been a photographer in East Berlin way before the Wall fell, and another, as a cultural institution, if people cannot dance, then at least they can come to see art.

It's getting near 10pm and Julia stands in front of the mirror in the hallway, and like rediscovering an old heirloom, she gets the old question out to ask herself. Honestly and deeply, is it about escape? Or is it to gain something that she can share back into the outside world? She decides the fresh breeze cycling along Hermannstraße through Kotti, then across the Spree, will do her good. The line is probably gonna be super crazy. She can just get there and see how she feels. 'And once I was in the line,' she says, the excitement was electric as people crammed together, they saw the lights go on inside Panorama Bar. 'This made me so happy. And so I decided this night I'm queueing just to have this feeling of going inside, of changing clothes, putting my stuff into the wardrobe, of when you walk in and you can look up eighteen metres to the ceiling and you already hear the sound of the floor and then you walk up the stairs . . .' The line-up has received criticism. Filled up with Ostgut regulars, stalwarts like Ben Klock and Marcel Dettmann, but then maybe after all this time, that reassuring feeling of providing a business-as-usual experience wins over any curveball for the venue to try something new.

'I remember the moment when it was 12 o'clock when the doors open,' Julia says, 'and people were cheering, which has never happened before.' The Berghain line is not the place to show emotion. You stand there, await judgement. 'I realised that I don't care how long it's gonna take to queue, I don't even need to dance. I don't need anything. I just want to have that moment. So yeah, I waited patiently for seven hours.' Seven hours of transitioning from the outside world is long even by Berghain standards. 'I always see it as something like a little meditation,' Julia says. 'I calm down and I'm just preparing into this state.' I think back to my own first time in the line, that snowy February in 2012, getting turned away, me and my temp Norwegian friends, from the minute the taxi dropped us off until we got to Sven, we made no attempt to transition. To disconnect. *Do you take your shoes off when you're a guest in somebody's house?* When I went back a week or two later, I just kept my head down, kept calm and got in. 'Maybe it's actually not so bad to have at least a little bit of a line because you stop thinking about all the normal stuff from the world and you have some time to get into a calm before you enter. Until you get those couple of metres before the door, because you're like, "Oh my god, are they gonna let me in or not? Am I smiling too much?" I actually realised that I like this moment where you have a transitioning phase.' The transition is something Julia is going through that night on her own. She notices people in front have arranged shifts in the line. Each swapping, holding a place, so the other can go pee or get food.

'And then once I was inside, I realised it exists exactly the way it always existed. I felt like I was coming home right away.' For the next two months, before rising corona figures drew clubs to close once more, Julia went four times. She noticed regulars from before alongside a whole new generation in their early twenties, too young before the pandemic. But things were, reassuringly, the same. 'And I know it always sounds a bit strange, but it really felt like coming home. This is the place where I feel like I can just truly be myself and relax. I can let go. I don't have to think about what other people are gonna think about me; it's like how you would feel in your own home when you can just relax on your couch and do weird stuff.'

Weird stuff.

'Like I remember going up and asking a very handsome guy: "Do you eat your snot still?"' Sonia Fernández Pan, writer, podcaster and curator laughs. I had read a piece Sonia had written for an online magazine, Coven Berlin, called 'Reassembling Histories by Putting them into Bodies that Dance', in which she expressed something I'd always felt but struggled to define. What she was writing about was to do with otherness in dance culture, how dancing is linked to the body and offers a utopian potential to express freedom, yet hierarchies emerge. This is what Ziúr was so careful about with her night, Boo Hoo. How inclusive can something be that has a dress code. In another part of the essay, she talks about how dance spaces simultaneously offer anonymity and community. But right now, we're talking about snot. 'And he was looking at me like, "What the fuck? Who are you?" But then, a while later he comes back to me and says, "Yes. From time to time, yes I do."' Sonia laughs again. She's in a room in Barcelona, spending the coldest month away from Berlin. She grew up dancing to drum and bass and listening to IDM and glitchcore in Valencia. A consummate record collector, she fell in love with buying vinyl in Berlin and, like Julia, has contrasting feelings about Berghain, about hierarchies that exist even within utopias. She has felt the judgement. One time in the line, she dressed in pretty office girl clothes, and it didn't matter she knew the music on the line-up intimately, security staff have been known to make quick judgements when they hear a Latin accent, and particularly a Latin-accented office girl. And turn her away they did. Until the security guard called her back once he saw her walking off, seeing her neck piercings. But then, we talk together about intimacy on the dancefloor. Intimacy through anonymity, and when Berghain is at its most yes. 'I felt super at home from the very first time in the way that I can be with people but I don't have to talk to them. I can be alone and together at the same time,' she told me, 'which is so relaxing.'

I say to her that when you go to meet friends for dinner, you bring wine or maybe a starter, and you're expected to bring a certain amount of attention. 'You bring your presence,' Sonia says. 'The degree of intimacy in dancefloor conversations, how you get to have very intimate connections with people where you share things that maybe you don't share with your friends. There are hierarchies in how people dance and also dancing too much is not so well seen, but you realise how important those people are that are there. You don't know their names, you don't know their phone numbers, but when they are not there in that club that you like to go every weekend, every month, whatever, you miss them so much. And that makes a scene.'

For Julia, who identifies as Queer but had spent most of her life in straight environments, this sense of a scene is connected to Berghain becoming a safer zone for her feminine expression. 'It's a safer space, the one place where I can truly be myself,' Julia tells me. 'As a woman, it's one of the few places where I feel I can express my sexuality without having to fear being objectified if I don't like it, or that I can be sexy but I know people will respect if I say no.'

'In heteronormative society, as a woman, you always have to be careful about men getting angry when they get rejected. Berghain gives me a sense of freedom for me to explore this part of myself without having fear. And it gives me a feeling of agency that, for once, I am in charge, I can show what I want and how I want it, and I'm the one who decides if I go anywhere with it or not.' She has a sweet spot, made up of three factors. 'Where's the best sound. So, I always follow my ears to where I think the sound is good. Then, the people around me, what's the dancing energy of the other people. And then if there's enough space, I need some space to dance.' She has a fondness of dancing in the middle in the back of Berghain, somewhere between the two boxes, where there's a fan coming from the top and the air is fresh, where the sound comes evenly from all sides. 'And then sometimes I wander around the crowd, usually a bit more to the left because I like the Gay boys' energy, especially when the techno is really hard. They always look at me as if to say, "What's this cute little girl doing here?" And then I'm really starting to dance and then they're like, "Okay, Okay. She can stay here!"'

I'm going to hold my hands up and tell you that I have not become a regular part of Berghain's family. I've enjoyed the times I've been; I've danced and lost myself. I agree in broad brushstrokes with the door policy, if that in keeping the level of scrutiny high, community inside is protected. There are few other places in daily life where the values of community win over, let's just say, commerce. Yet I also see this as a trade-off, too, between protecting community and making judgements that can never entirely be accurate. The last time I went, inside dissolved slowly into the outside world of forest and Krumme Lanke, I swam between dragonflies, the reedy water filling my nostrils. But my visits were less and less frequent, and by the time I'd moved to the city, my wavelength had transitioned somewhere else.

When I was sharing thoughts back and forth with Julia, she was on holiday, I think she said Lisbon, but the wind distorted the phone signal. She told me she had been dancing, two nights earlier, in a club called LUX, and that on the woman at the bar's T-Shirt was written: Music Is The Answer. *Musik Ist Die Antwort.* 'For me,' Julia reflects. 'I see it more as proof that there are actually quite a lot of people who would like to live in a society that is more open and more diverse; I see this in the way people treat each other in this place. It gives me hope that actually all these people who go there and who enjoy that people are treated with respect, and that they can be free and non-judgmental, that maybe they have a little seed inside of them and I try to take this back into the real world. If all of us go from Berghain into the real world and we spread this little seed of friendship and respect, maybe there's a chance for a better world. In Berghain, I realise that I'm not the only person who would like to live in a society like this.'

10.

ECHOES IN THE EAST

MARK REEDER. EAST BERLIN.
PUNK. BLUES MASS.

'If you think Berghain is bad, you should have tried getting into East Berlin.' Mark Reeder stirs his café macchiato with a long thin spoon. Just now, as we walked into the cafe and ordered, the barista heard his accent and asked where he was from. 'Manchester,' he says and she lights up: 'I knew it, I'm from Manchester too!'

The two start gassing about home, about old clubs; she says he reminds her of Hacienda DJ Dave Haslam. Mark tells her he knows Dave and that he's visiting in a few weeks. She asked how long he's been in Berlin. 'Since 1979,' he replies. 'I just came here to buy some records, and I never left.'

Last summer, when Mark and I had walked around Schöneberg, where he'd first arrived on that warm, drizzly night in 1979, I listened to echoes of the anarchic, free and creative eighties, the *Genialer Dillitanten* through his words. A roar of the *Dillitanten* echoed a few months later and a few kilometres north, where I next caught up with Mark in a submerged former crematorium in Wedding. He was DJing the closing party of an exhibition detailing in vividly stylish artworks, old magazines and film footage, the music, art and ice-cool attitude of all-female bands Malaria!, Mania D and Matador. Centred around Beate Bartel, Bettina Köster and Gudrun Gut, these nexuses were industrious in appearance – starring down from giant photographs on the exhibition walls in blazers, trousers and boilersuits, they kept their hair short and their expressions full of intent.

They were industrious in sound – often dissonant, always strident, frequently (but not always) singing in German. They found a way with electronics when most of their male counterparts worldwide were still caught up in the tangle of their guitar strings. Malaria!'s 1982 EP *New York Passage* is minimal, propulsive, angular, futuristic, dubbed-out in places, and Mark was their manager. When I arrived that night, I could hear Mark's set from the other end of the building. Playing at around 110bpm. Playing big, echoed out remixes he'd made for New Order, Anne Clark and Depeche Mode. I noticed Gudrun Gut at the bar, holding a cocktail, her jacket folded over her arm. To me, she's as iconic a post-punk femme as Kim Gordon. I wanted to introduce myself, but I became overcome with shyness.

It's now February 2022. I woke up to an air of uncertainty. Instagram feeds from friends in Kyiv are a mixture of business as usual and fear. Russian troops gathering on the borders by Ukraine. This morning, Mark sent me via WhatsApp a track he'd made with Lithuanian-based singer Alanas Chošnau. 'As the threat of war looms on the European eastern front,' he'd written, 'I thought it would be important to write a song with Alanas that reflected the situation through the metaphor of lovers/friends splitting up.' Mark's connection to the east pre-dates Berlin. Once, he'd smuggled cassettes into Prague in 1978, a precursor for the role of *Subversiv-Dekadent* he'd play across the next decade and across heavily patrolled borders.

I get the feeling that to a lot of West Berliners in the eighties, what happened on the other side of the Wall was like a phantom, a ghoul half seen in the mirror. There's a section in *B-Movie* where Muriel Gray asks Blixa Bargeld if he ever thinks about going to the other side. He provokes her that he's gone to the other side many times, but not the other side of the Wall. Why would he want to go there? Three days into living at Winterfeldstraße 24, the apartment that was to be demolished but that never was, Mark was living above West German students and he asked them how he too could get to the other side. 'Impossible,' they told him. 'You don't want to go there.' The students' dismissiveness wasn't too dissimilar from the reactions he'd received as a hitchhiker travelling through Cologne, through Dusseldorf, through Munich, when he'd asked about visiting West Berlin. Again – why on Earth would you want to go there?

'It was the fear of the unknown,' Mark tells me, taking off his green jacket and hat, 'but this made me even more curious to go.' We move into the café's seating area, where grey light shimmers in from a window opening out onto a small, tree-filled *hoff*. On other tables, a few people are working on laptops. The music is calm, pleasant coffee shop indie, Beirut or something. 'And I was convinced I'd seen how to get there in a Europe-on-$5-a-day-book, these travellers bibles that hippy people had. I found one in a junk bookshop on Potsdamer Straße and it said to go to Checkpoint Charlie. Just by chance, as I left the shop, this sports car pulls up and this guy says, "Do you know where the Brandenburg Gate is?" And I've just been there, and I was like, "Yes, I know where it is. Do you know where Checkpoint Charlie is?" And he knew.'

'And so I thought, I'll just go for the day and have a look around.' Since its construction, Checkpoint Charlie has been that most cinematic a shorthand for the Cold War. A visual prop for the protagonist of every spy film to face a moment of searing tension. Here, usually, an American or English citizen involved, perhaps unwittingly, in espionage will cross over to the other side after being faced down by brutally expressionless guards. Checkpoint Charlie was off-limits to both West and East Germans. Only military personnel and members of the fourth power pact: Americans, French and British, like Mark, could cross. The surrounding Friedrichstraße, a grand yet desolate trench.

'It was like a petrol station without pumps,' Mark recalls. 'There were huts and these red and white barriers to guide you towards them, and in the middle, filling the entire width of the street, this massive tower. You could see the silhouettes of the border guards up in the top with machine guns and binoculars, watching the west.' He'd encountered the seriousness of border controls arriving through the Iron Corridor into the walled-in west three days earlier. As a hitching passenger, he got out of the car to pay his five marks transit visa to expressionless guards and their suggestive machine guns.

He realised there were places with unknown consequences. 'If I fuck up here, I have no idea where I could end up, maybe some gulag breaking stones for all I know,' Mark tells me. 'As Brits, we're constantly cracking jokes and doing daft things, even with authority. I had this realisation that you can't joke with these guys.'

'With Checkpoint Charlie, you had your passport control. They'd then look at your passport, look at everything, and then you'd go through customs control. But inside the huts, they'd wallpapered and stuck up photographs of paintings of Brandenburg from the 1800s. It was all Formica and potted plants to make it like this fake home, this fake cosiness. Imagine something like Wallace and Gromit's spaceship. They'd look through all your pockets and make sure how much money you were taking in, and you'd have to write it down on a piece of paper, a declaration of what you were taking in with you. Are you taking a camera? You couldn't take a cine camera in. You could take a normal camera in, take still photos, you could do that, but taking a cine camera in was a no-go. You couldn't take a cassette player in like a Walkman. The East Germans made you exchange your West German marks at a rate of 1:1 for East German marks when the real exchange rate was more like 1:10. And the money had to tally when you came out, so you couldn't go in with twenty West Marks and come out with ten because they'd say, "Where did the ten go?" And then they'd give you these freshly printed DDR banknotes in a little thin tracing paper envelope like stamp collectors have. Everything was monitored. You were registered the minute you walked through the gate.'

Over the next ten years, crossing through Checkpoint Charlie, as well as just up the road at Friedrichstraße U -Bahn, Mark would learn the impracticalities of concealing vinyl and the best way to disguise the give-away rattle of cassettes. And he would learn that, if you were lucky, you might just get through without a kind of search. 'But they'd be watching you, watching your body language,' he says. 'Have you maybe a roll of 25,000 East German marks stuffed in yourself?' But for this first time, before he would learn the true forbidden nature of music, Mark learnt that the very final millimetre of the Western world was made up of a white, painted metal, mesh gate. It was here where he stood as the last border guard checked his documents, he heard a buzzing. The gate opened. He was in East Berlin.

Now, where Checkpoint Charlie's one remaining hut stands is a cultural shift between Kreuzberg and a stretch of Mitte overwhelmed in both global commercialisation and the com-mercialisation of history. Near where a heritage sign lets you know you that you're now leaving the American sector is one of the city's comparatively few McDonald's. In the spy films, this is where our protagonist will be intercepted by a waiting car, or where, out of the desolate ruins, our protagonist will get their luxurious Western jacket stolen by malnourished Eastern delinquents. For the hero of our musical journey, there wasn't a car or another human to be seen. The stretch was desolate. 'It was like being in some kind of like sci-fi movie where nobody's there. I'd only walked maybe a hundred yards and this copper comes out of nowhere.' Mark takes a sip of his coffee. 'I showed him my passport. And as I was walking down this street, in almost every other doorway, there was a cop on both sides. And I thought because you're really close to the border, there are gonna be a lot of these coppers hanging around, they're really here, really watching everybody, but there was nobody to watch.'

He walked. Like every British kid of his age, he grew up fascinated by the war – his parents had fought in it – yet as he walked past the quarter where Hitler's bunker was, where the propaganda ministry had been, he'd presumed these had all been destroyed by bombs. He walked past buildings cordoned off, grand and classical buildings towards *Unter den Linden* and the east side of Brandenburger Tor, realising as he walked why the Russians wanted East Berlin rather than the west. 'Because it had all the best bits, these classical buildings, it looked fabulous.' He saw people now. People on the streets. He took note of his Western clothes, definitely something to bear in mind for future visits if he didn't want to stand out.

He saw people driving Trabants, the small, state-monopolised cars, heard the tak-tak-tak sound they make. 'It sounded like a moped encased in a car shed and they spewed out petrol fumes – the smell! I remembered going to Yugoslavia in 1976 and there were a lot of Trabants and they had the same smell. I thought that petrol, that must be the smell of communism.' He saw the robotic precision of goose-stepping soldiers guarding classical buildings. Mark walked upwards towards Alexanderplatz and the TV tower. He noticed the CCTV cameras, positioned on rooftops, three metres long with huge lenses. 'They filmed all of Alexanderplatz to see if anybody was going to protest, to do something anti-state. If you were a kid with a placard that said, "I hate the DDR, Kill Honecker", within about two and a half minutes, you'd be removed.'

It was lunchtime now, and under the Fernsehturm he saw the queues of people waiting to get into a canteen. 'There was some kind of smell like school dinners,' Mark says. The canteen was simply called SB. *Selbstbedienung*, meaning self-service. 'And inside, these dinner ladies were ladling out slops, like braised pork in gravy, potatoes that looked like they'd been cooked about 15 million times and dried out. I was like, I'll have some of that salad, chopped carrots, red and white cabbage. It tasted like it'd been washed in Domestos. The cutlery was made of aluminium, as was some of the money in the DDR; it was really light and I wondered: if you put a two mark piece on the top of a coffee, would it float? And I was looking around and watching all these people tuck into the meals; I was thinking, this is their lunch break and they're enjoying it. If you've grown up with this and this is all you've known, then it probably tastes perfectly normal. Because I'm from a different world, my taste buds have developed in a completely different way. It was an enclaved world. I couldn't take a Western cookbook to the DDR because they'd see all these things that they couldn't eat, all these exotic things like fresh peas. I was wondering what they would think if they could eat my food.'

Where we're sat now, in Nothaft Cafe, just across from a raised green viaduct that runs along Schönehauser Allee, was once part of the DDR. The U-Bahn station outside once called Dimitroffstraße, named after Bulgarian communist leader Georgi Dimitroff. Like its namesake, who was rumoured to have been poisoned in 1951, Dimitroffstraße is no more. Now, the stop is Eberswalder Straße, the very same straße I had last exited on my way to meet DJ Fuckoff a few months earlier. It's easy to take for granted that the modest luxuries we're sipping would've been unthinkable only a relatively short timeline ago. 'I discovered later,' Mark says, 'that they really had more or less everything that we have, but it was all their versions of it, their interpretations. I remember when their Walkman came out and it was like a brick; it wouldn't fit in any pocket, took about twenty batteries and cost about two and a half grand.'

1979 becomes 1980. In the West, as the scene across Schöneberg and Kreuzberg was developing out of bars, cafes and boutiques, where art and chaos were intermingling and the Wall acted as a playpen for subsidised creation, Mark was leading a double life. After that first visit, he went back every day for a week, and then these visits carried on regularly. 'I was trying to find stuff,' he says, curious to see if there was some kind of scene, any like-minded music souls within this strange alternative reality. I picture this section in a spy film; it's the section where our protagonist journeys alone, covers his tracks, looking for signs, until one day, when Mark meets a kid on the train. 'He was wearing a pair of drainpipes and had a bit of spiky hair, and I thought, "I bet he knows where there's maybe some kind of new wave-type bands playing." He got off the train, and I ran after him and said, "Do you know anywhere?" And he says, "There's nothing. There's no punk rock. It's all forbidden." They listened to punk off the radio, and that's it. I knew they couldn't telephone into the West, so I gave him my address and said, "If you hear of anything happening, write me a postcard and let me know." And I didn't hear anything from him. At all.'

'And then, a couple of months later, I get a letter from this girl asking to meet me at Palast der Republik, the former parliament building.' The futurist splendour of Palast der Republik had giant golden windows that looked out across Mitte, and inside, a round cocktail bar equally as stunning. It was known as The People's Palace. 'It looked like a set from Stanley Kubrick's *2001*. And she said, "I'd like to meet you, can you come over on one of these two days? I'll be there, I'll wait for you."' Mark sat on an orange leather seat in the bar and waited. The lush surroundings not concealing his thoughts that he knows he's a Western interloper on a covert mission inside East Germany's parliament, waiting for an unknown contact. He feels unsure if and when she'll turn up; he's unsure who she could turn out to be. Maybe she's a spy, a honeypot on a mission to curtail his coded information. When she arrived, she was in her early twenties, wearing a leatherette jacket, scarf around her neck, self-dyed black jeans and an *Unknown Pleasures* T-shirt.' 'Her hair had blonded tips,' Mark says, describing this first meeting with Kerstin. 'If her hair had been green or blue, she wouldn't have made it anywhere near the Palast der Republik, let alone up in the cocktail bar. She kept it kind of new wave, but at the same time safely fashionable enough to be tolerated in the DDR. She sounded me out, asked me where I'm from, what I'm doing, what do I want.' Kerstin and Mark would become friends, just friends, a part of him aware of the dangers in doing so. As the kid on the train had said, 'There's no punk rock, it's all forbidden.' He knew what all East German's knew, that anyone could be spying for the Stasi. As it turned out, Kerstin would become an important collaborator, taking excessive risks to her life and wellbeing before later escaping the DDR. 'She was the person who introduced me to her circle of friends, the fledgling punk/new wave scene in East Berlin.'

The scene had to operate covertly; they held parties in their houses. Mark learnt more about why there seemed to be no punk concerts, no new wave. 'You had to apply for permission to possess an instrument,' he explains. 'And then you had to apply for permission to play it, and then you'd have to audition in front of a panel. The panel was made up of some group of blokes, all blokes, guys who don't have a background in music. They were all former heroes of the working class, miners, steelworkers. They'd assess your proficiency as to whether you could play your instrument properly and whether you would get the coveted permission to actually own an instrument and play it in front of an audience. It was really hard to even start a band. If you managed to get a guitar from, say, a flea market or something like that, and actually start a band, the minute you started, if anyone found out what you were doing, you were under the observation of the Stasi.'

'Then you'd be controlled. Because that was the whole point. They're not gonna have you jumping up spouting anti-socialist, anti-state paroles from your music and attracting a lot of young people. They'd say, "Let's see your lyrics! What's this about?" They'd be looking out for . . .' he says in a whisper, emphasising the paranoia, 'subversion!' The cafe, for a second, is silent. 'That's why they were so fearful of punk, because it was exactly that. Whereas rock music, they'd reigned that in at a pretty early stage. For ages, I went to gigs in East Berlin. I had a look to see what was happening there; the bands were state-regulated. They were all dressed in jeans and playing blues and progressive rock stuff, drively, tepid versions of Free. I just thought, there must be something else. There is nothing else.'

Officially, punk couldn't exist. Having a subversive nature immediately made punk an enemy of the state and a total no-go for the committee's decision to grant a music licence. But then again, just about the least punk thing a punk could, or still can do, is seek permission from authority. Check. Punk was illegal and 1980 became 1981. Mark made other DDR friends, his Eastie friends, he calls them. All the time, he covered his tracks, making sure, for their own safety, that they didn't know about each other. He sussed how to prepare cassettes for smuggling, the way to wedge material around the case, between the tape-heads, blocking their pocket rattle that could be a giveaway to the border guards. On the cassettes, he'd make mixes of everything he could think of. Film soundtracks. Synthpop like New Order, Soft Cell and OMD. New albums and their accompanying maxi-singles. He'd fit on the B-sides. 'It became a ritual making the tapes for my Eastie friends,' he tells me. 'Eventually, I ended up having this idea.'

One afternoon in a bar, a hippy was sitting at the end of a long trestle table; he was listening in to the conversation. 'He says to me, "You're not from here, are you?" because my German was so bad, and he was amazed that someone from England would be in East Berlin. We got talking about music; he liked things like Bob Dylan. He told me that he had an electric guitar and that he played, but he didn't have permission, so he played in the church, at a so-called Blues Mass, and I'm like, "What's a Blues Mass?"'

One blustery winter afternoon in late 2021, I walk back to where I spent that very first weekend in Berlin, where, in trudging in snow back from Lidl along Rigaer Straße in Friedrichshain, I had stopped to look up at the grand, gothic splendour of Samariterkirche. Today, almost a decade later in my own personal Berlin timeline, I meet Monika, who is waiting for me at the corner of Samariterstraße and Bänschstraße. Monika is tall, bespectacled and keeps her hair in an androgynous quiff. We look up at the church and she explains to me what a Blues Mass was. 'Some people in the church opened the doors for punks because they saw these young people have many problems. Punks on the street were hunted by the police almost every day,' Monika tells me. We stand drinking takeaway coffee. Now in her late fifties, she remembers how a small handful of places gave refuge to East Berlin's underground punks and that she was one of them. 'But it was only a few churches, for example here or in Lichtenberg. And they had their own room to meet and to talk to each other and to organise concerts. It was like an isla as it was impossible for the police to go into the church and take out the punks because there was an agreement between the church leaders and the communist leaders.' The agreement was partly based on the Catholic church's size and influence, the Communist Party afraid to get in the way. Instead, they chose to monitor.

'So this hippie guy in the bar is telling me about the Blues Mass,' Mark tells me. 'I didn't realise at that particular moment just how precarious it was for him to actually be doing this until I started to do it myself. Then I realised this is a different world. There aren't that many bands and the few that there are, they're silent.' The seed was there: could he smuggle a band from the West across the border to play for his Easties? 'I actually played a gig in Prague in 1982 with Die Unbekannten. It was the first illegal gig ever in Czechoslovakia by a Western new wave band. They had Western artists perform on telly like Boney M but secret gigs by unknown bands were not done. And I'd met these dissidents and we did this gig disguised as a wedding reception in this farmhouse on the outskirts of nowhere. And Czechoslovakia's most wanted, all these dissidents turned up: Plastic People of the Universe, Jolly Joker, and we all get completely sloshed and did this party, and at that time I wasn't so aware of how significant it was. So, having had this experience of actually performing in Czechoslovakia, which was even more draconian, in a sense, than in East Berlin, I thought maybe we could do a gig in a church.'

1982 in the West, Mark was managing Malaria! He was punk band Die Toten Hosen's sound engineer. Mark had his own band, Die Unbekannten, who, in new wave circles, were early adopters of synths and drum machines. Die Unbekannten were the first band to record with a Roland 606. The cassettes to his Eastie friends kept coming, but the idea of smuggling across a band wouldn't go away. Originally, he wanted to bring across Die Unbekannten, but there were problems. If you thought smuggling a cassette across either Checkpoint Charlie or Friedrichstraße was risky enough, how about smuggling a synth? He realised that all of their instruments would have to be sourced from East Berlin. 'But nobody in East Berlin had a synthesiser,' Mark tells me. 'The biggest East German acts, like Karat, they might have had one, but these kids in East

Berlin, they certainly didn't. Nobody even had synthesisers in the UK. You could buy a cheap guitar with your dole money, I think it was a month's wages, but synthesisers were astronomical. It was the privilege of your David Gilmours. Very few bands, even the big-name bands, had synthesisers. But West German bands had synthesisers because they were all bloody rich. That's why I was so much into German synthesiser music.' The economic miracle really helped the development of *Kosmische* music, of Kraftwerk, of Tangerine Dream. But in East Germany? 'A synthesiser was like a spaceship. They'd never seen one, let alone buy one.'

Mark thought the next idea was to put everything on a cassette as a backing track, but nobody would lend him a cassette player. 'Because in East Germany, they cost around two thousand marks. When your average wages were about six hundred marks a month and your rent maybe twenty marks, it was dead expensive, so it was something people didn't necessarily want to give up straight away. What happens if we get raided by the Stasi? The police come and everything gets confiscated. And then in the end, I gave that up.'

1982 into 1983. In Mark's spare room, an Australian with big hair called Nick Cave was licking his wounds after the dissolution of his first band, The Birthday Party. 'I was on tour with Die Toten Hosen, and I'd taken all their cassettes into East Berlin because they're sung in German and I knew that my friends there would be really into them. Then I spoke to the band and said, "If I can arrange it, would you be interested in playing in East Berlin?" They were like, "How are you going to do that? It's impossible. But if you can arrange

it, we'll do it." Mark worked with Kerstin and her friend
Jackie, but first, he had to warn them. 'I told my friends
initially when we were planning this gig, if you get caught,
your lives will change forever. If I get caught, I'll never come
back; they won't let me back in. The only thing that you're
going to miss is me bringing cassettes in, whereas for you,
your lives will change forever because you'll be blacklisted
and your lives will be miserable. And I don't know what the
consequences of doing such a thing as an illegal gig would
be, but it had never been done before, so probably it'd be
really harsh just to make an example of you all.' Kerstin and
Jackie, however, were unequivocally on board. 'I think maybe
that was a bit of the attraction behind it for them, the thrill
of it. Because I went into East Berlin every week, smuggling
cassettes in, I had that thrill every time I went in, this thrill
of elation of actually going through this rigmarole, this cat
and mouse game of trying to take all this stuff illegally into
East Berlin. Hopefully, the customs wouldn't strip search me
and find it. Whereas they didn't have that in their daily lives,
they had it differently. With the Stasi knowing that anybody
could potentially be an informer, they had that. But this,
the thrill of actually doing something against the state, they
didn't actually have that. That, and the fact that they were
punks. It's the cherry on top of the cake. It was like, here's
your opportunity to have that feeling of elation, the thrill of
arranging something completely anti-state and totally illegal.
I asked them, "Do you really want to do this?" and they were
like, "There's no discussion, we don't care what happens, they
might even throw us out of East Germany."'

March 1983. They found the church. Erlöserkirche in Rummelsberg. They invited thirty people. Whilst the equipment was being sourced in the East, Mark and the band had figured out how to cross the border at Friedrichstraße. 'Getting in, it was a bit like getting into Berghain again,' Mark says. 'Breaking up a big group of your friends into little groups of two or three to get through. We thought, if you go in a big group, they'll become suspicious. So we staggered our way through. No one acknowledged that they knew each other.'

'We did this gig. The whole time, I was thinking, the Stasi could come at any moment, kick the door in and we'd be all arrested. And the suspicion of who within the circle of friends we had invited could be a Stasi informer, you never knew. So that's one reason why we only invited thirty people, because we wanted to diminish the risk of how many people, and these were all so-called "trusted" friends. And we said, no photographs. I took my camera, but I only took two photographs, the priest took two photographs, that was it. No photographs during the concert. As it turned out, years later, I got to see the Stasi file, and other people got to see their Stasi files who were part of that scene. We discovered some people had actually taken photographs. In fact, one of the people who was one of our closest, trusted friends was actually a Stasi informer. But they wanted to see the gig, and one thing I realised afterwards, they didn't inform on any of the gigs or any of the activities before they happened because they wanted to actually experience them. If they'd have told the Stasi in advance, then the police would have definitely been there and that would have been it, game over, no gig. So, in their reports, it would be something like, "I only found out about it a few hours before it actually happened, and I went, and there was no time to make a report prior to the gig."'

'The other reason why I wanted only thirty people is because I wanted to be like the Sex Pistols in Manchester, to have that significance.' Mark refers to the gig on 4 June 1976 that only thirty people attended. Amongst these were people who were forming or would go onto form Joy Division, The Smiths, The Fall and the Buzzcocks. 'I wanted it to be a sort of German version of that moment. Not that I expected that of the thirty people, half of them form bands like what happened in Manchester. It was about the implications of doing such an event, what it would mean to all the kids in the DDR. I wanted to give them hope, embolden them somehow and to show them that you can dream and your wishes could be fulfilled.'

There is so much more. A book more. But we've drunk our coffee and it's time to go. There would be one more time he'd smuggle Die Toten Hosen across, into a church in Pankow in 1988. Recently, I'd received a WhatsApp from Mark, asking if I was free, and if so, could I meet him at Vinetastraße U-Bahn station at 3.30pm. Something too secret to reveal in an encrypted text would be happening. I got there and we had walked along a leafy suburban straße to the church from 1988, Evangelische Hoffnungskirchengemeinde, where a congregation formed outside. There were middle-aged ladies with pink and green hair, grey-haired guys with punk T-shirts, suave media sophistos and punk kids. It was the thirty-third anniversary of this last illegal Blues Mass, under the noses of the Stasi, just over a year before the Wall would fall. Acid house was already sweeping across the underground a few kilometres west. Die Toten Hosen played as we sat on church pews, the singer had taken on the late middle-age good looks of a TV doctor, Mark had a bottle of water and paper cups to offer around like a picnic. At this gig, thirty-three years earlier, there were fraught happenings. Maybe a story for another time, just as maybe we'll talk about MFS, initials that once represented East German Ministry for State Security: the Stasi. How Mark hijacked these initials to mean Masterminded for Success. Whereas the city reconnected, he worked with Ellen Allien, Cosmic Baby, Dr Motte, Effective Force and Mijk van Dijk. Or how one Monday morning, a young Eastie warm-up DJ called Paul Van Dyk turned up at his office. But for now, we leave the shop. I'm off to jump on the U-Bahn at the former Dimitroffstraße station. The girl from Manchester and Mark banter. We say goodbye and he says, 'I'm Mark.' She says, 'Yeah, I know who you are.'

11.

ALLES GUTE ZUM GEBURTSTAG

ROBERT BENNETT. SISYPHOS.
PSYCHEDELIA. SOUTH AFRICA.

Five minutes until the set begins. Robert reaches the booth. He stops. Again, dizziness rises. Decades of practicing bodywork, a lifetime of yoga has given him an athlete's physique way past retirement age. But then two weeks ago. Bam. Out of nowhere, waking up in intensive care on a drip. The doctors informing him he'd suffered a cerebral haemorrhage.

He really shouldn't be here, but he breathes deeply and climbs up into the booth. On his back, a rucksack with his laptop, controller and headphones. He could have died so easily, the doctors tell him, but then, Robert might well reply that he's never existed anyway. A lifetime of meditation, experiences outside of the body. Did something just say, 'No more'? Was it that recent second Pfizer jab? Of course, he's wondered this, laying up in recovery, but then, here he is. The dizziness, it'll pass, he hopes, and he takes a moment to focus on the breath as a kick drum vibrates across the bellies of dancing bodies and brings him back into the present. And that present is that it's almost seven on a Monday morning and Robert Bennett is about to play the closing set in Sisyphos, and he thinks, 'Am I going to make it?'

Over the night leading up to this moment, Robert dozed, never entirely sleeping. He can never entirely sleep before a set. Instead, he lays in bed, keeps still, does breathwork. He knows what it is to be in the present. As a boy in a homeland that would later exile him, his grandmother practised Buddhism. She studied in monasteries and started teaching him meditation when he was seven years old. He knows what it is to be still, that the body is an instrument for understanding the mind and the mind is an instrument for understanding the body, and together, they are both instruments for what lies beyond understanding. Bodywork has been the core of his existence even before arriving in Berlin forty years earlier. He's a doctor of sorts and has seen internal revolutions in people who have come to him. He's cured racists of racism, but right now, there's this terrible disassociation, that feeling of dizziness. There is sunlight outside, and in the booth, there is a DJ who has cued up their last track and in less than a few minutes, Robert is expected to take over. Christ, that's got to be 130bpm, he thinks.

Four minutes until the set begins. Through the night, his housemate Shakti had friends in her room. It was her birthday and they were being so conscientious that despite the thinness of Neukölln walls, he barely heard their music, barely noticed their conversation. For Robert, DJing was an unexpected late gift. 'Book me before I die' runs his SoundCloud contact details. How many people start their careers playing across some of the world's best floors in their late sixties? But that's what happened. You run a breathwork workshop and put together a mix. Some of your clients like the mix and turn out to be club bookers. So what do they do? They ask you to play. And what do you do? You're flattered and you say yes. After all, music has run deep your entire life. Whether that's waking up one morning to see Phil Lynott asleep on your living room floor or the throbbing of psychedelia that has existed in different forms over different generations. So, they book you, and low and behold, you're playing on a boat, and do you know what? You're really fucking good. And then what? They book you for Sisyphos. This was several years now and Sisyphos, this big post-apocalyptic party just east of the ring, has become a home. This morning at 3.45am, the alarm went off. Robert got up, took a shower, had something to eat. The bag with his laptop, his controller, his headphones are waiting by the front door like a faithful dog outside Lidl. In her room, Shakti and her friends blow out candles, they put on their coats and scarves, somebody takes a few olives and wraps them in tissue for the ride. East of Ostkreuz in a taxi, along Hauptstraße, the dawning sun rising over buildings as they approach the arched gate between the industrial east and the party inside.

Three minutes until the set begins. In this compound of warehouses and huts, once a dog biscuit factory, sweat and techno fill the air. It's really rather unpleasant – the brain fog, the dizziness. 'Can I actually do this?' he thinks. Can I actually play these next three hours? The bookers have given him a barstool, so he can sit as he plays. He sits on it right now, nose inches from vinegary perspiration collected around the neck of the outgoing DJ's shirt who has unplugged their headphones and is twisting EQs on their one remaining track. Robert shuts his eyes and breaths deeply. Half a century has now passed since the night LSD spoke to him. In a flat in Knightsbridge, Robert was self-destructive, lost in the disillusioned end of the sixties. She told him, 'Robert,' she said, 'you're going to have to do this without me now.' 'How?' he asked, scared to lose his greatest teacher. 'You know,' LSD replied, 'you've always known.' So then, as now, he becomes present.

Two minutes. 'We love you, Robert,' Shakti and her friends shout. They are dancing at the back of the *Halle*. It's Monday morning and people are getting up to go to work elsewhere. However, in this space, where soundwaves travel across the mirror balls that hang down from the ceiling and through and into bodies, the outgoing DJ is now tweezing the filter, reducing the kick drum, minimising. Robert is cueing up; he checks the LEDs. He was right. 130bpm.

It is just about 7am. Some have been inside here now for over a day. When I first visited one Easter Sunday, I was with a couple of friends and, moving from room to room, we found a garden shed in the middle of a dancefloor. We climbed inside and, for a totally unspecified amount of time, had a private party. The dancefloor we were sitting in the middle of disappeared. I was living in London at that point and I can remember initially feeling that, at any moment, a security guard would poke their head inside and tell us the shed was off-limits. After a while, we left anyway, another group took our seats. Sisyphos is the yang to Berghain's ying. There is none of the latter club's sleek minimalism. Here, people dress in various colours and dance underneath a menagerie of lampshades and birdcages. Before I left that time, I sat on a torn sofa and watched the sun rise across the Spree. But right now, It's 7am on Monday 18 October 2021. Pioneer lights hovering below Robert's eyes, the last eight bars of the outgoing DJ's kick drum exit the room like a fly out of a summer window. Robert releases his hand.

Voices fill across the *Halle*. Children singing in German. Voices haunted through reverb and underpinned by a single hi-hat. Shakti smiles; he's playing it! Decades earlier, Robert's daughter and her friend returned from kindergarten and sang. Robert jumped up, inspired to capture this moment. He had a four-track cassette recorder. Cables ran across his home studio, headphones on, the two girls singing into a mic. He shouts, 'Again!' Double-tracked. Triple-tracked. Abbey Road, yes! The cassette goes into a box of other cassettes. TDK, BASF, titles and dates written in biro. Archived for well over a decade. 'Somebody wrote it as a counter-thing to happy birthday and it never really caught on,' Robert says to me, stretching into himself, several days of stubble protruding from his chin. 'But it's a nice song, a bit of an earworm, actually.'

We're in his kitchen. It's just over twenty-nine hours after he began playing and he tells me, whilst pouring boiling water into two mugs, that he hasn't been up too long. The air is fresh, surfaces are clean, there is no visible evidence of an afterparty that only wound down recently. 'My daughter was really into singing in those days,' he says with a little bit of a wobble. We walk through to his bedroom, where his studio is set up. 'She was with a friend who was really gifted musically; they had said, "We've learned this new song" and she said, "Can I sing it to you?" I said yes, so they sang it, and I said, "Woah, that's lovely, let's record it" and they thought that was really cool, these two eight-year-olds sitting in a studio with headphones on double-tracking themselves,' Robert laughs warmly. His daughter is now a digital nomad living in Mexico, her childhood voice recorded decades earlier echoing through the speakers of Hamma Halle, serenading his housemate's birthday and signalling in the last set on a Monday morning. 'And a few years ago, I sent the track to a friend for his birthday, who just happens to be one of the bookers in Sisyphos. He put it on SoundCloud. He loved it and a lot of DJs asked me if they could have it.' He pauses. 'Sorry, you'll have to ask my daughter. She has the copyright.' Did she give it? I ask. 'Yes, she did; she thought it was really funny. She loves the idea of her being played in Sisyphos,' he roars. Robert has a way of roaring with laughter as if it offers a suggestion to something beyond, deeper, like a psychedelic punchline.

This is the third time I've drunk black tea in his apartment, but the first since the pandemic. I ask how he is, and he says, 'Spaced.' That's when he tells me about the cerebral haemorrhage. He says almost, by the way, that he could become dizzy, disassociated at any moment. He says this as if offering me an apology for what he's been through the last two weeks. In his studio, we sit on chairs framed under a mezzanine. In front of us, hanging percussive instruments: a tambourine, a cowbell, some wind chimes. A large desktop opened up on Ableton cued up with a recording of yesterday's set taken from the club mixing desk. The last time I was here, he played me a mix he'd made of The Beatles' Stockhausen-disco mantra Tomorrow Never Knows, gently nudged and stretched out by hands so adept to the untangling of bodily tension.

On stage and on cloud, Robert Bennett becomes Robot Bennett. A human cyborg assisted by an APC 40 Mk II controller. Before this unexpected autumnal happenstance that led to his cybernetic alter-ego playing dark techno onto the floor of Gretchen, of Jonny Knüppel, of Mensch Meier and of Rummels Bucht, local night-time staples in Berlin, he'd been a lifetime hobby musician. In swinging London, he was a troubadour with an acoustic guitar, a bummed out outcast living with a bunch of hippies; his housemates even sold weed to Mama Cass, who'd stay from time to time in the flat above. And even now, sometimes, not as Robot Bennett but as Robert Bennett, he will DJ what he calls the music of his youth: classic psychedelic rock from the sixties and seventies. He recalls one New Year's Eve when he even played these sounds in Sisyphos. For Robert, psychedelia has always acted as a guiding force for change, but the methodology of change has altered through time. He once told me that he might never have become a hippie or a rebel if he'd grown up in a peaceful country with human rights. 'I'm not even talking about an ideal society,' he said, 'but a society a lot better than South Africa.'

Born on 4 February 1949 into what he could sense even before he could understand was a terrible cloud. 'My parents told me it was something to do with the country we were living in,' he says. The previous year the Afrikaner National Party had won the general election, bringing with it apartheid, literally meaning 'apartness' in the Dutch-German-French coloniser language of Afrikaans. 'I was picked on by other white children because most of them supported apartheid,' Robert says. 'My family was very much against apartheid. My brother-in-law was very active, and he got raided by the security branch at five o'clock in the morning. In the typical sort of way they'd do things, several times he got put in prison.'

His mother was a member of Black Sash, a women's organisation that stood against the regime. His father was active in the Progressive Party, the only left-wing party recognised and permitted, the Liberals having been banned. 'From that time on, I was incredibly aware of the injustice going on in the country, the abuse of human rights. It made me more aware of what was going on in the rest of the world: the civil rights movement, the Vietnam War and, most importantly of all, the Cold War.'

When Robert was thirteen, Kennedy and Khrushchev faced off over the Cuban Missile Crisis, which, he says, 'made me feel that all life could be snuffed out at any time by a nuclear war.' The threat of nuclear extinction would decades later play a decisive factor in why this nomad stopped and settled in Berlin. Robert opens a window. His body is tall, fighter-lean, offset by the natural deep-furrowed lines of a septuagenarian. This is how Hemingway imagined men, I think.

'I went to university and possibly far too quickly became influential in the student union, who were arranging protests against apartheid.' Robert was nineteen. 'I became a member of the national executive in my first year at university, the first freshman and the youngest student ever to achieve that.' It was 1968. 'And, of course, you remember what happened . . .'

Around the world, the protest movement galvanised. Inspired

by the momentum of the Paris riots, students across America protested the war in Vietnam. Here in West Berlin, Marx-studying radicals mobilised out of Freie Universität demanded an end to the right-wing controlled media, full of old Nazis, still there, still in positions of power. By 1969, the African National Congress had been outlawed for nearly a decade and Nelson Mandela had already spent several years on a prison island. In the urgency of the late sixties, Robert began to reject the liberalism his parents clung to. What use is it to lobby when all it takes is one finger on a button to end it all? 'And I told my father, there's nobody to vote for. Your stupid party is totally middle of the road.'

Suddenly, keys jingle in the doorway. '*Hello, ich bin hier mit Paul,*' Robert says outwards towards the hallway. Shakti, the birthday girl, has arrived, bringing in a cold breeze, the smell of fresh bread and a cough from the Turkish market. 'We're closing the door because we're recording,' he says, leaning his head towards the hallway. 'Shame, I'd love to hear,' Shakti replies, popping her head in between the gap. I say I'm totally fine with her being present if Robert is. She smiles and says she'll join but will first prepare a sandwich.

'Where was I?' Robert says. I hear a cough in the kitchen. Raver's cough, not corona cough, I think. 'Of course. BOSS.' There was a particularly eventful protest. Robert got arrested and taken to a police station. 'And the security police, they were really called BOSS: the Bureau of State Security.' BOSS. 'And boss was the word that every black man was supposed to say to a white man: "Yes, boss", "No, boss."' Robert was accused of hitting a BOSS. 'I didn't touch him!' He holds a hand up as if in confession. But a confession accompanied by another of his deep, cosmic laughs that seem to vibrate across the whole room. 'And I said, "You can't hold me, I'm a British citizen and I want to see my consul."' The BOSS man spoke. Robert summons up a most thuggish Afrikaaner accent: '"Mr Bennett, either you leave the country, or something's going to happen to you or your family, especially your niece." My niece was three years old at the time, and they had killed people that I knew. I had to get out of there. After I left, they killed my ex-girlfriend with a letter bomb and her three-year-old daughter, who was next to her. It was a long time ago but that's how this disgusting fascist regime held onto power. I thought I couldn't go and fight and kill these bastards. So I left and went and drowned my sorrows in London in a haze of drugs.'

'I just decided the world is fucked, so all I want to do is get high. London was swinging. London was really swinging. In a way, I'd have rather stayed and continued my political activism, but realising that would only land me in prison, or dead, like quite a number of my friends. I thought it more prudent to escape and enjoy just becoming a drop-out.' He moved around a lot, finally ending up in the basement of a flat in Knightsbridge, living in the crumbling remains of a once-prosperous property full of what he calls crazy hippies, with a London-visiting Mama Cass on the stairwell and Phil Lynott's hair poking out of a rug one morning. 'Thin Lizzy slept on our floor when they came over from Ireland once. They didn't have anywhere to stay. One of our hippie mates met them in a park and brought them home.' I think of *Performance*, the film directed by Donald Cammell and Nic Roeg, where a building in a similar part of London during this disintegrating era becomes a gateway for merging identities and a jumping-off point of the sixties dream. I ask if Thin Lizzy were nice people. 'Yes,' he says, without hesitation. 'They were very well behaved. I saw one of Zeppelin's very early concerts and Jimmy Page blew me away. He took an acoustic guitar and sat down three meters away from me in the break, but I was never a fan of Zeppelin. They had that huge, lush sound. Hendrix had this too, but Hendrix was more interesting to me because he was black and had a feminine side. I lived like that for a couple of years, played guitar, played in coffee bars, played folk music, and put the anti-apartheid thing behind me. But I was a drop-out. I never felt part of society. Because I and many colonials in those days, we had felt this feeling, even if we weren't, of being English.'

'I was born in South Africa. My mother was born in Rhodesia, as it was called in those times. Her father came from Ireland and her mother was the only one of my grandparents actually born in South Africa. We felt that we were more English than the English. So I went to London and expected to find this country that would welcome me as one of its own, but I found exactly the opposite. I was treated as an outsider, even within the hippies and freaks and drop-outs.' I ask if he thinks this was a class thing. 'No, I knew lords and ladies selling heroin and working-class people too. In any case, I was never treated as English.' Around this time, Robert confesses that his outlook became more nihilistic. Already affected through experiences in South Africa, the tick-tock of nuclear war and then the denial of being fully accepted in the English counterculture.

He found relief through experimenting with LSD. 'We had a little group of people with whom I was associated,' he says. 'We tried to do it in a way where we thought of it much more as consciousness-expanding rather than just having fun. We never did it at parties or festivals. We always did it in a safe, small group, and we did it infrequently. But after my fourth trip, she said to me, "Listen, you have to try and find these states on consciousness without me." I said, "How?" and she said, "You know. You've been doing it for years."'

Shakti pops her head around the door and whispers if she can borrow Robert's phone. Robert reaches for it off a table where it sits charging alongside a row of small hard drives on a white cloth, lined up neatly like ceremonial amulets, which, if as I imagine they contain tracks for sets, then I guess they are. I ask her how the market was. 'A little intense to begin with,' she tells me. She runs off to the kitchen; being out seems to have jumpstarted her batteries. We hear a plate dropping, followed by 'Oh fuck it, *shizer*.'

Robert left London and travelled to India, following the hippie trail. 'As it is now called,' he says. 'We didn't call it the hippie trail and we didn't call ourselves hippies. We called ourselves freaks. My grandmother was a Buddhist and she taught me to meditate when I was seven years old. She had stayed in monasteries and through her, I got interested in zen, non-duality and yoga. I went to India to reconnect with this. I alternated between living in Goa with all the hippies, where I was smoking my brains out from morning to night, and then going to India. I say going to India because we didn't see Goa as India. Goa was like this enclave. And then I'd go back to

India and live in an ashram. Exactly the opposite, no drugs at all, meditation and yoga. I was learning Vedanta with a guru, learning Hatha yoga with another guru.' He's still active ten to twelve hours a week doing workshops, doing what he describes as working with traumas that have externalised into people's bodies. He even managed a little of this last week in his recovery. 'I find yoga classes take too much energy now. I'm too old for that.' He lets forth another of those laughs that I've now come to wait on, like a train of comfort. I get the feeling India embedded something in Robert that I can feel in the room now. Something that has fuelled an energy that means even now in his seventies, only two weeks after a cerebral haemorrhage, he could more than scrape through a 7am set in a techno cave but turn it into some kind of communion, a birthday party and a goodbye to the weekend. Since playing, and touch wood here, he tells, me, his symptoms are largely gone. India re-channelled his energy. 'I had changed my mind from thinking that I can change the world from the outside to thinking the best way to change the world politically is to help people change themselves,' he explains.

Sisyphos is one of Robert's homes. An adopted dancefloor space that in many ways birthed Robot Bennett. There have been others since he arrived in Berlin: The Love Parade. People whom he got to meet at parties after Love Parades and the transient families they'd forge across the festivals, like Fusion and Nation. And in Kit Kat Club. This is the nineties. When Robert and his first wife came to Berlin in 1982, they found a home within two weeks on Goltzstraße, the one and the same straße in Schöneberg where I took a walk in the summer with

Mark Reeder. The same straße where Mark showed me echoes of the emerging underground scene emanating through bars, cafes and boutiques. At this time, Robert was aware from the peripheries of the *Geniale Dilletanten* and its players – The Birthday Party, Neubauten, Malaria! – but priorities had changed. 'My ex-wife, we met in England when I was doing my body therapy training. We fell in love and came on holiday to Berlin a couple of times. She had lived here before and I thought, "What an amazing, crazy city",' he laughs. Before they settled, there were various twists and turns. He mentions time spent in California, but that time is not important for our conversation. 'And so then, we decided to try Berlin.'

'But there was another point for me coming here and this takes a little bit of explaining. Because I was born in 1949 and because I was in puberty during the Bay of Pigs and the Cuban Missile Crisis, I thought the world was going to explode. I was living in South Africa and I thought, "Okay, it's gonna take a little while longer before it gets here. We'll live a few days longer. And, of course, because of apartheid, and after I was thrown out of South Africa, because of that, I felt like a rootless, homeless person in this world. I was pretty pissed off. Pissed off with capitalism. Pissed off with communism. So I thought, "I'm not going to live in either. I'm going to go and live in the middle in between West and East, which is Berlin. When the nuclear war breaks out, I'll be the first to die because they're gonna level West Berlin first, and I want to go as fast as possible with it when it comes."'

In the West Berlin of 1982 that Robert arrived and settled into, divvied up into four quarters like a political Monopoly board, one quarter each for the victors of the Second World War, Schöneberg was, like Kreuzberg and Neukölln, under American occupation. There were huge demonstrations nearby Goltzstraße on Winterfeldplatz from time to time. They'd see people streaming down the street covered in blood after being beaten up by police. Occasionally they'd join demos. Occasionally, too, they'd frequent the bars of the scene, but the couple's focus was firmly in establishing themselves as therapists, working intense hours and building up clients.

A previous time I'd visited, sat where we are now, in front of his monitor, he'd played me a remix where he'd taken the 1970s Krautrock of Can's already mesmeric track 'Spoon' and massaged in a deep 4/4, full of subtle dub filters and echoes. I love the original like an old friend and, listening to how he'd subtly fostered it into something that he plays at Sisyphos, it felt like a natural connecting point between all of the psychedelia of his musical timelines. The sixties he lived through and the dark techno of his metamorphosis as Robot Bennett collide into one. When he first heard techno, though, through his son, Robert was resistant. He was living in England in the early nineties and he was a DJ, organising parties, and he brought this music on cassettes, which I couldn't stand,' Robert laughs. 'I never liked his music and this was the worst, this computer music, end of the eighties, Detroit stuff.' But finally, after being forced to listen by his son, one track became an earworm. 'And he laughed at me and said, "Ah, I've caught you." And he gave me that cassette, and then I started asking him for more. And then I heard about this parade which was going on, this demonstration which was celebrating this music, and I thought I'd go along and have a look. I'd never been to a techno club and I'd never seen people dancing to it.'

'And when I went to the Love Parade, the first thing I thought was that the hippies are back. Strange music they're listening to, but the hippies are back. They were all bright and colourful and had this same kind of vibe.' The switch that Danielle De Picciotto and Dr Motte activated only two or three years earlier when monochrome became technicolour across the Ku'Damm was still years away from when the pulse would pull in over a million people gathered in euphoria around Tiergarten's Siegessäule. Out of the dour, speed-fuelled end of the eighties, new flowers were blossoming out of cracked paving. 'Being a hippie,' Robert explains, 'I was very disappointed when the freaks stopped being freaks, which happens with every youth movement, of course, but you don't realise that. You think this can go on forever.' The psychedelic era had returned. Psychedelia, as a way of transformation. The trance state of the dancefloor and the trance state of Robert's work in therapy. The revelation from India, where Robert had changed from thinking he could create change from the outside to thinking the best way is to help people change themselves. These personal transformations, micro-explosions, happening through trance, and he says, 'The quickest and most effective way I can transform is through dance.'

Shakti has entered. She sits on a chair next to us and places a plate of cream cheese on fresh market bread on her knees. We all pause. There are comedowns present, emotions and energies settling. Robert clicks the mouse. We watch orange blocks of waveform on the monitor.

We hear the voices. Timelines converge, a blur of moments.

Is this bringing you back? I ask. 'Yes, so much,' Shakti says. She looks caught in emotion, hearing back her birthday. We hear Robert's daughter, her friend, singing into a four-track recorder decades earlier. Their voices recorded so near where we are now in Neukölln. Now, a hi-hat, a synth bass, whoops and cheers of dancers caught in yesterday morning. Robert clasps her hand, a rush reopened. The window is open.

12.
A STAND-IN FOR PARADISE
DAVID JAZAY. LOW. HÖR. COMMUNITY.
KREUZBERG. HASENHEIDE.

Berlin is two cities that exist in the same body. In the summer, it is a forest. In the winter, when temperatures drop and the leaves on the trees fall away, it becomes the skeleton of a grainy 16mm film. On Schlesische Straße, I notice as I chain my bike against a rail where an unknown artist has tagged the word CLIT, in the winter, tags replace trees.

CLIT hovers everywhere. On doorways, on U-Bahn escalators, on shutters. From Moabit to Marzahn. A friend in Neukölln had been told by a friend that the artist was a man. Possibly an abbreviation of his name and not, she told me with a sense of genuine disappointment, a feminist slogan. For years before I moved, I'd visit Berlin only in the winter months. I loved the bareness. It was Bowie living off red peppers and milk as he made *Low*.

A friend, the London-born DJ Hannah Holland, had lived in the city for a while and described to me the bleakness she felt listening to *Low* as she was walking through a freezing January

Alexanderplatz to buy hoover bags. She described this to me with a shudder, before saying that, however, in the summer months, Berlin transforms into the best city in Europe. I didn't mind the bleakness. It wasn't until I moved here that I discovered the joys of the lakes in summer, the beauty of cycling home in a T-shirt post-club in the fresh morning light. However, I still have a special romance with the cold, bare streets and I find myself going back, indulging in *Low*, where songs just fade out as if, by chance, they were made in a city still bombed and ruined. Yet, songs that at the same time contained whole sonic vignettes. In mellotrons, I saw seventies wallpaper. I draw into a seventies Berlin I never knew.

Outside a cafe, smoking a roll-up with his headphones on, is David Jazay. We bonded, in part, on a shared love of this bleakness within Bowie's Berlin trilogy. 'Even if in subject matter they might be gloomy,' he once told me, 'and it's slightly depressive like *Low*, through all of that I always heard the joy of creating something new, a new sound, a new beginning.' David is tall and speaks with a gentle Bavarian English that is sometimes more English than the English. He moved to Berlin specifically because he wanted to record an album, admiring the work of Bowie, Iggy and Eno. Like so many, he too thought he'd only be here a couple of years. Twenty-five years later, where we meet, along this strip in Kreuzberg, is still his *kiez*. 'I have a very personal relationship to this area,' he tells me as we walk. 'Because when I was a young boy, I was here with my dad. We went to the end of the street, just fifty metres from here where the Wall was standing, and we went up on one of those looking platforms and looked over.'

We go past the work of another tag artist. Roy draws uni-corns with captions inside like Fuck Off, Gay and Happy and You Look Nice. We walk through tourists. David is a musician, filmmaker and teacher, and his photographs of Dublin from the 1980s capture another lost time. As a child, he was too young to have a political sense of what he was looking at over the Wall, but the memory lingered. Then, in the mid-nineties, it became home. 'This street was so amazing,' he tells me. 'It was so empty of cars, and there were the Turkish greengrocers. The international flavour, that was very impressive to me at that age.' Where we are now is a history of club culture itself. This strip, where one end breaks off into Treptow, then shoots past us before morphing into Köpenicker Straße and lead-ing all the way for a further 2.5 kilometres until it runs out into Märkisches Museum, all the while flirting its way along-side the Spree like two future lovers at a bar. From Club der Visionaire and Chalet at the Treptow end to Watergate near us, and then on to Kraftwerk and Kit Kat and even that most early, pioneering vault, UFO. But back in 1995, David recalls, 'everyone was going, "Yah why don't you move to Prenzlauer Berg? Kreuzberg is not hip. There were so few bars, which is hard to imagine now. One hundred years ago, there would have been even more bars, cinemas and ballrooms. After the fall of the Wall into the first decade after it, right until the time I moved here, there was only one bar, but I only went in to get cigarettes from their machine.'

'It was really easy to get a flat,' he laughs. 'You'd be by your-self and you'd say, "Ok I'll give you two days' notice." You'd go to a cafe and think about it, sleep on it, and then you'd call them and they'd be super grateful. Even ten years later, people were actually offering you places to rent; they couldn't even rent them out.' When we first met, it was a hot summer evening and a friend had invited me to a film screening in a small empty shop space near Görlitzer Park. The screening was of a film, *Fliegende Ratten*. Rats with Wings. A film David had directed, that had been shown in competition, then lost in time. It was a rare print of a film that nobody saw when it came out, but it left a strong impression on me. It dealt with life amongst drug addicts in Görlitzer Park and was shot, Vérité style, within the nature of the city.

The film felt as if it was made in a forest. 'Most of it is set here in Görlitzer Park and I very much thought of this place as a stand-in for paradise,' David tells me as we take seats in a bar, Sofia, that he frequents. 'I always hated the cliche that cities are cold and isolating and that you're really lonely because you're in a city. I think the opposite is true, and I didn't want to go down that way of saying, "Yes, brutalist architecture makes people depressed." In the film, whenever they go to shoot heroin, they go to these beautiful little ponds with ducks and sparrows.' During the screening, the real location of the film was just outside. It was balmy hot, vest at night weather and people were kicking it. We drank outside a *Späti* after, and I cycled home drunk. Reality and 16mm converging, this time during the summer months. Far away from my *Low* listening and visualising.

As the seasons change, things get thrown up. An axis shift. Flies that have survived into October drunkenly hover closer to surfaces. Intense lunar-style activity. I cycle past an entirely naked man, naked except for a briefcase, along Karl-Marx-Allee. His briefcase and penis swinging with steady purpose, as if being late for a meeting. Who's to say he wasn't either? Trees clear, you'd never know they were there. Hidden wrinkles, rashes, bruises and dried blood of Berlin's history is easier to see.

Behind a fencedoff tenement house sentried either side by skips brimming with bricks and a warning sign that reads *Betreten Der Baustelle verboten. Eltern haften für ihre Kinder.* Children are banned from the construction site. Parents are responsible for their children. I am in the sleepiest end of the no longer neglected Kreuzberg and cycling between the chic eateries of Graefekiez and the grande dame of all SO: Bergmannkiez. Sandwiched between lies Südstern. A village. A *dorf.* A couple of straße like an inner-city village green staggered with antique shops. The kind that only sells beautifully refurbished DDR-era lamps and is only open during certain days. Where organic ice cream parlours, florists and Turkish-owned hookah bars have stretch limo pink and black interior seating. And Hör Radio. Hidden behind the sign that reads *Betreten Der Baustelle verboten* is a room with a fish-eye camera lens angled towards a toilet-like DJ booth. This is where Hör Radio, a streaming service, like a static Boiler Room, has risen. Hör's rise coincided with the pandemic.

When a thirty-something pulse, a pulse that has evolved in tempo, in oscillation, in the hands that control the pitch and the ears, feet and hearts that dance but that has fundamentally not stopped since the fall of the Berlin Wall, suddenly stops, catapulting DJs and promoters and dancers into every kind of uncertainty, makeshift churches were made immediately. United We Stream, a collective of streams of DJs playing from empty clubs, organised by Berlin's Club Commission, started as early as 13 March, before the bars even closed. Suddenly, where taking photographs had been forbidden, Facebook was now sending people weekend pop-ups of static CCTV-style cams from inside these previously off-limits subterranean worlds. We all became the ancient, ancient Rose in Titanic, viewing the empty interiors of worlds we once knew. Hör Radio, barely a year old when the pandemic began, provided a lifeline for DJs who suddenly found themselves without dancefloors.

Dancing in a streaming booth is one thing; dancing in a field is another. Other churches appeared, churches that didn't need a roof or moral consent. I cut across the rubble and meshing of Hör Radio's driveway south into the green meadows of Hasenheide. Past the smell of sheep and fowl in the petting zoo and up across the higher pathway. African *Ausländers*, denied work rights, are forced into selling weed out of economic necessity and operate in a collective, standing in and out of the bushes and trees. Beyond, beyond the nudists in the FKK area. Freikörperkultur. Free Body Culture. The nudists have, in recent times, squeezed in to make way for the up-all-night ravers deprived of club space during the pandemic. It's a Sunday, and in Hasenheide, people are sitting in clumps under trees, a few small sound systems still going strong. There are wine bottles on the path I swerve around. A yoga class. I stop, climb off the bike and walk into the field.

You can hear them first. A group of elder folk under a tree are playing instruments, guitars, bass, a trumpet, and a synthesiser.

Facing inwards, listening to each other, playing for the love of playing. Guitar and synth arpeggiators synced together, oscillations echo out from duelling guitarists. Birds in the tree above sing and then fly across where, in the deep distance, I see the TV tower. The musicians have that thing that comes when a group of people play together for some time. Like dancers in the sweet spot. Like DJs who've just entered the automatic. Like the wordlessness of community.

SPECIAL THANKS TO ALL THOSE WHO PRE-ORDERED THE BOOK

Ryan Amrabadi, Luca Andriollo, Gemma Anthony, Anton Ardakov, Barbara Barbieri, Daniel Beck, Steve Beck, Brian Belle-Fortune, Sandira Blas, Michael Brown, David Campion, Shane Cashin, James Cator, Olivier Chanut, George Clarke, Martijn Deijkers, Nick Delaney, Edward Dowie, Orla Doyle, Peter Drabwell, Yvonne Duffield, Bass Dye, Sam Evans, Tim Forrester, Jacqueline Forward, Barbara Fraser, Oli Freke, Finn Glendon, Kate Glover, Marge Goymer, Thomas Greatorex, Timothy Hammond-Evans, Penny Hanford, David Harvie, Sebastian Heit, Thomas Hnatiw, Karin Hollingsworth, Mark Holmes, Paul Jobson, Shane Johnston, Elin Juhlander, Russ Kemp, Simon Kemp, Lucy Korenke, Holly Lester, Daniel Lewis, Allan Little, Claire Madit, Mufeed Mahmood, Peter Mallett, Kevin Marshall, Tim Matthews, Steve McLay, Simon Messer, Blair Millen, Joerg Mueller-Kindt, Wiebke Nörenberg, Estela Oliva, Sergei Pozhidaev, Mark Quail, Tom Ralph, Damien Ratcliffe, Mark Rayworth, Chris Reed, Fabien Riggall, Dan Roberts, Kerrie Robinson, Jaime Rosso, Martin Ruddock, Sarah Ryan, Pablo Smet, Jes Sewerin, Gregory Smith, Jonathan Steele, Dave Stoffell, Tena Strok, Leigh Strydom, Clara Suess, Christina Taka, Michele Tessadri, Randall Thompson, Pete Thornton, Jon Turner, Pete Willes, James Wilson, Phil Wistow, Mark Wood, Thomas Wykes

ALSO ON VELOCITY PRESS

JOIN THE FUTURE
BY MATT ANNISS

Since the dawn of the 1990s, British dance music has been in thrall to the seductive power of weighty sub-bass. It is a key ingredient in a string of British-pioneered genres, including hardcore, jungle, drum & bass, dubstep, UK garage and grime. Join The Future traces the roots, origins, development and legacy of the sound that started it all: the first distinctively British form of electronic dance music, bleep techno.

STATE OF BASS
BY MARTIN JAMES

As UK government legislation, standardised music and bad drugs forced the euphoria of the rave into the darkness, a new underground movement emerged – jungle/drum & bass. Drawing on interviews with some of the key figures in the early years, State of Bass explores the scene's social, cultural and musical roots via the sonic shifts that charted the journey from deep underground to global phenomenon.

FLYER & COVER ART
BY JUNIOR TOMLIN

Showcasing the mastermind behind some of the most iconic rave flyers and record covers of the late eighties and early nineties, Flyer & Cover Art is a comprehensive insight into Junior Tomlin's incredible back catalogue. It is the first time his work has been documented and presented in such a comprehensive, cohesive fashion.

BEDROOM BEATS & B-SIDES
BY LAURENT FINTONI

Bedroom Beats & B-sides is the first comprehensive history of the instrumental hip-hop and electronic scenes and a truly global look at a thirty-year period of modern music culture based on a decade of research and travel across Europe, North America, and Japan. Combining social, cultural, and musical history with extensive research and over 100 interviews, the book tells the B-side stories of hip-hop and electronic music from the 1990s to the 2010s.

BOOK TWO
BY THE SECRET DJ

In this hilarious, gripping and at times deeply moving follow-up to the smash hit first book, the mysterious insider pulls no punches, wryly lifting the lid on misbehaving stars, what really goes on backstage, how to survive in the DJ game, and where the real power lies in rave. Above all, they chart how capitalism bought and sold the utopian dreams of the Acid House generation - and whether those dreams can still be saved.

SYNTHESIZER EVOLUTION
BY OLI FREKE

Synthesizer Evolution celebrates the impact of synths on music and culture by providing a comprehensive and meticulously researched directory of every major synthesizer, drum machine and sampler made between 1963 and 1995. Each instrument is illustrated by hand, and shown alongside its vital statistics and some fascinatingly quirky facts.

WHO SAY RELOAD
BY PAUL TERZULLI & EDDIE OTCHERE

Who Say Reload is a knockout oral history of the records that defined jungle/drum & bass straight from the original sources. The likes of Goldie, DJ Hype, Roni Size, Andy C, 4 Hero and many more talk about the influences, environment, equipment, samples, beats and surprises that went into making each classic record.

LONG RELATIONSHIPS
BY HAROLD HEATH

Written by former DJ/producer Harold Heath, Long Relationships is a biographical account of a DJ career defined by a deep love of music and a shallow amount of success. From the days of vinyl, when DJs were often also glass-collectors, to the era of megastar stadium EDM, it's a journey of 30 odd years on a low-level, economy-class rollercoaster through the ups and downs of an ever-changing music industry.

TRIP CITY
BY TREVOR MILLER

In the summer of 1989, when Trip City was first released with a soundtrack by A Guy Called Gerald, there had been no other British novel like it. This was the down and dirty side of London nightclubs, dance music and the kind of hallucinogenic drug sub-culture that hadn't really been explored since Tom Wolfe's The Electric Kool-Aid Acid Test. Maybe this is why Trip City is still known as "the acid house novel" and an underground literary landmark.

THE LABEL MACHINE
BY NICK SADLER

The Label Machine is the ultimate guide to starting, running and growing your independent record label. You will learn all about the music industry business and how to navigate the tricky dos and don'ts.

DAFT PUNK'S DISCOVERY
BY BEN CARDEW

Daft Punk's Discovery is a homage to a fascinating, troubled beast of an album that casts a huge shadow over the 21st Century. It's a global view of Discovery as a cultural phenomenon, placing the album at the centre of celebrity culture, fan clubs, video, the music business etc., while also examining its profound musical impact.

TAPE LEADERS
BY IAN HELLIWELL

In the form of a richly illustrated compendium, Tape Leaders is an indispensable reference guide for anyone interested in electronic sound and its origins in Great Britain. For the first time a book sets out information on practically everyone active with experimental electronics and tape recording across the country, to reveal the untold stories and hidden history of early British electronic music.

THE SECRET DJ PRESENTS
TALES FROM THE BOOTH

Tales From the Booth raises the BPM, rounding up an all-star cast of Secret DJs to tell their anonymous stories of what it's really like to rock dancefloors for a living. From strange encounters on tour to side-splitting debauchery and afterparty excess to the seamy and even dangerous side of the industry, this is your access-all-areas backstage pass.

DREAMING IN YELLOW
BY HARRY HARRISON

Written by one of DiY's founding members, Dreaming in Yellow traces their origins back to early formative experiences, describing in detail the seminal clubs, parties, festivals and records that forged the collective.

FRENCH CONNECTIONS
BY MARTIN JAMES

Drawing on a dazzling array of exclusive interviews with the biggest names in French electronic music history, French Connections: From Discotheque to Daft Punk - The Birth Of French Touch explores France's significant contribution to dance music culture that paved the way for the French Touch explosion.

OUT OF SPACE
BY JIM OTTEWILL

Out of Space plots a course through the different UK towns and cities club culture has found a home. From Glasgow to Margate via Manchester, Sheffield and unlikely dance music meccas such as Coalville and Todmorden, this book maps where electronic music has thrived, and where it might be headed to next...

MEMBERS ONLY
BY ROB FORD

Members Only is a showcase of the iconic membership cards and passes (VIP, Access All Areas, etc) of the acid house and rave generations. In A to Z format, the book features over 500 items of memorabilia from the late 80s and 90s and covers all the legendary and pioneering events of the eras.

VELOCITYPRESS.UK/BOOKS